CAMBRIDGE
UNIVERSITY PRESS

Chemistry

for Cambridge IGCSE™

ENGLISH LANGUAGE SKILLS WORKBOOK

Richard Harwood & Timothy Chadwick

CAMBRIDGE
UNIVERSITY PRESS

University Printing House, Cambridge CB2 8BS, United Kingdom

One Liberty Plaza, 20th Floor, New York, NY 10006, USA

477 Williamstown Road, Port Melbourne, VIC 3207, Australia

314–321, 3rd Floor, Plot 3, Splendor Forum, Jasola District Centre, New Delhi – 110025, India

103 Penang Road, #05–06/07, Visioncrest Commercial, Singapore 238467

Cambridge University Press is part of the University of Cambridge.

It furthers the University's mission by disseminating knowledge in the pursuit of education, learning and research at the highest international levels of excellence.

www.cambridge.org
Information on this title: www.cambridge.org/9781108948357

First edition 2022

20 19 18 17 16 15 14 13 12 11 10 9 8 7 6 5 4 3 2 1

Printed in Italy by L.E.G.O. S.p.A.

A catalogue record for this publication is available from the British Library

ISBN 978-1-108-94835-7 English Language Skills Workbook with Digital Access (2 Years)

Additional resources for this publication at www.cambridge.org/go

Illustrations by Tech-Set Ltd

We would like to thank Fiona Mauchline and Sally Burbeary for their valuable contributions to this book.

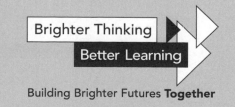

> Contents

> How to use this series

We offer a comprehensive, flexible array of resources for the Cambridge IGCSE™ Chemistry syllabus. We provide targeted support and practice for the specific challenges we've heard that students face: learning science with English as a second language; learners who find the mathematical content within science difficult; and developing practical skills.

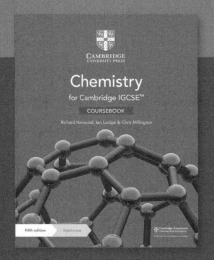

The coursebook provides coverage of the full Cambridge IGCSE Chemistry syllabus. Each chapter explains facts and concepts, and uses relevant real-world examples of scientific principles to bring the subject to life. Together with a focus on practical work and plenty of active learning opportunities, the coursebook prepares learners for all aspects of their scientific study. At the end of each chapter, examination-style questions offer practice opportunities for learners to apply their learning.

The digital teacher's resource contains detailed guidance for all topics of the syllabus, including common misconceptions identifying areas where learners might need extra support, as well as an engaging bank of lesson ideas for each syllabus topic. Differentiation is emphasised with advice for identification of different learner needs and suggestions of appropriate interventions to support and stretch learners. The teacher's resource also contains support for preparing and carrying out all the investigations in the practical workbook, including a set of sample results for when practicals aren't possible.

The teacher's resource also contains scaffolded worksheets and unit tests for each chapter. Answers for all components are accessible to teachers for free on the Cambridge GO platform.

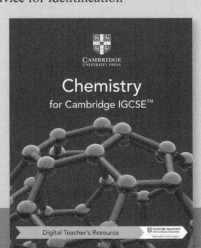

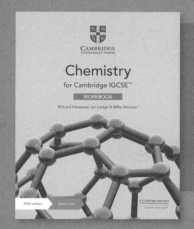

The skills-focused workbook has been carefully constructed to help learners develop the skills that they need as they progress through their Cambridge IGCSE Chemistry course, providing further practice of all the topics in the coursebook. A three-tier, scaffolded approach to skills development enables students to gradually progress through 'focus', 'practice' and 'challenge' exercises, ensuring that every learner is supported. The workbook enables independent learning and is ideal for use in class or as homework.

The practical workbook provides learners with additional opportunities for hands-on practical work, giving them full guidance and support that will help them to develop their investigative skills. These skills include planning investigations, selecting and handling apparatus, creating hypotheses, recording and displaying results, and analysing and evaluating data.

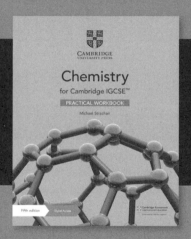

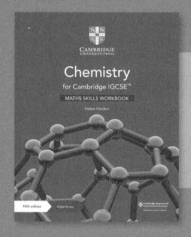

Mathematics is an integral part of scientific study, and one that learners often find a barrier to progression in science. The Cambridge IGCSE Chemistry write-in maths skills workbook has been written in collaboration with the Association for Science Education, with each chapter focusing on several maths skills that students need to succeed in their Chemistry course.

Our research shows that English language skills are the single biggest barrier to students accessing international science. This write-in English language skills workbook contains exercises set within the context of Cambridge IGCSE Chemistry topics to consolidate understanding and embed practice in aspects of language central to the subject Activities range from practising using the passive form of the verbs in the context of electrolysis to the naming of chemical substances using common prefixes.

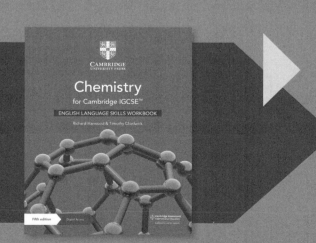

> How to use this book

Throughout this book, you will notice lots of different features that will help your learning. These are explained below.

INTRODUCTION

This sets the scene for each chapter.

LEARNING INTENTIONS

These set out the learning intentions for each exercise. Each exercise will help you to develop both your English skills and your Chemistry skills.

KEY WORDS

Key vocabulary and definitions are given in boxes at the start of exercises. You will also find definitions of these words in the Glossary at the back of this book.

Exercises

These help you to develop and practise your English skills alongside your Chemistry skills.

LANGUAGE FOCUS

These give you more information about parts of the English language that you may find challenging, to help you use English more fluently.

LANGUAGE TIP

The information in these boxes will help you complete the questions using correct English, and give you support in areas that you might find difficult.

> Supplement content

Where content is intended for students who are studying the Supplement content of the syllabus as well as the Core, this is indicated with the arrow and bar, as you can see on the left here.

> Introduction

Welcome to this workbook, which will help you with your study of Chemistry using English. To make good progress in your studies in Chemistry, it will help if you can also use the English language well in a way that is appropriate to science. If you can read English well, you can understand what is written in your Chemistry coursebook easily. If you can write and speak English well, you can share your knowledge about Chemistry with others easily.

This workbook will help you understand some important topics in Chemistry. It will also help you develop your skills in English. The exercises will give you practice in both things at the same time.

The exercises will help your English skills in different ways. They will:

*   help you understand the meaning of important words

*   help you to use certain types of words correctly, like nouns and adjectives

*   help you to construct sentences correctly

*   help you to construct whole passages of text

*   give you practice in reading text and extracting information from it.

The areas of English covered in this book have been chosen because they are useful to understand and discuss the subject of Chemistry. Aspects of language are discussed directly to help you understand certain exercises, and to explain why these aspects are useful to you as you learn Chemistry. There is also a Skills and support section at the start of this book that provides an overview of the English language skills covered. You can refer to this section at any point to help you find out more about the language skills discussed within the chapters. You will be able to link these explanations to the content of your English language course.

We hope you enjoy using this book, and that it helps you progress in your studies of Chemistry and English.

Note for teachers:

Additional teaching ideas for this English Language Skills Workbook are available on Cambridge GO, downloadable with this workbook and the Cambridge IGCSE Chemistry Teacher's Resource. This includes engaging activities to use in lessons, with guidance on differentiation and assessment.

Answers to all questions in this English Language Skills Workbook are also accessible to teachers at www.cambridge.org/go

> Skills and support

Introduction

This section includes information about English language skills which are essential in order for you to understand science concepts and to communicate your science ideas effectively to others.

You can use this English reference section at any time to support your studies in science.

Quick reference guide

Grammar	Use	Example
noun (n)	A word to show the name of a person, place or object.	a *chemist* a *classroom* a *chemical*
verb (v)	A word to show an action or state.	I *explain* the reaction taking place We *understand* the process
adjective (adj)	A word to describe the quality or state of a noun.	The *flammable* organic solvent The *reactive* compound

Verbs

We need verbs to describe the action of a substance changing state, or of the person (also known as the agent) doing the action. For example, the verb *to boil*:

The water *boiled* to form water vapour when the temperature reached 100 °C.

Remember to use the correct form of the verb:

Present simple for facts: Water *boils* at 100 °C.

Past simple for a finished past action:
In our experiment last week, the impure water *boiled* at 103 °C.

Present simple

The present simple is used to talk about facts and things that are generally true. It can also be used to talk about habits and routines and often with verbs of senses and perception, for example: *think, hurt, understand.*

There are different groups of verbs in English, for example, the verb *to be*, regular verbs and irregular verbs.

The verb *to be* can be used to describe somebody or something and can be followed by adjectives and nouns.

	Affirmative	Negative	Question
I	am	am not	Am I ...?
he, she, it	is	is not	Is he, she, it ...?
you, we, they	are	are not	Are you, we, they ...?

Example sentences:

Affirmative	Negative	Question
I am a student.	I am not a student.	Am I a student?
It is a molecule.	It is not a molecule.	Is it a molecule?
They are elements.	They are not elements.	Are they elements?

Regular verbs in the present

In sentences with *I*, *you*, *we* and *they*, use the basic verb form. For example, *tell, read, say.*

In sentences with *he*, *she* and *it*, you must add -*s* or -*es* to the end of the verb.

With verbs ending in a consonant (b, c, d, f, g, etc.) + -*y*, change the *y* to *i* and then add -*es* in the affirmative form when it follows *he*, *she*, *it*. For example, *it flies.*

When the verb ends in -*ch*, -*ss*, -*sh*, -*x* or -*zz*, also add -*es* in the affirmative form when it follows *he*, *she*, *it*. For example, *she watches.*

With verbs ending in a vowel (a, e, i, o, u) + -*y*, add -*s* when it follows *he*, *she*, *it*. For example, *he stays.*

	Affirmative	Negative	Question
I, you, we, they	I study chemistry on Wednesdays.	I do not study chemistry on Wednesdays.	Do I study chemistry on Wednesdays?
	We understand the formula.	We do not understand the formula.	Do we understand the formula?
	They react with oxygen.	They do not react with oxygen.	Do they react with oxygen?
he, she, it	He studies chemistry on Wednesdays.	He does not study chemistry on Wednesdays.	Does he study chemistry on Wednesdays?
	She understands the formula.	She does not understand the formula.	Does she understand the formula?
	It reacts with oxygen.	It does not react with oxygen.	Does it react with oxygen?

Irregular verbs in the present

Some verbs are irregular, meaning they don't follow the usual rules. Some examples of irregular verbs are *have*, *go* and *do*.

	Affirmative	Negative	Question
I, you, we, they	I have a formula.	I do not have a formula.	Do I have a formula?
	They go into the laboratory.	They do not go into the laboratory.	Do they go into the laboratory?
	They do calculations.	They do not do calculations.	Do they do calculations?
he, she, it	It has got a formula.	It has not got a formula.	Has it got a formula?
	He goes into the laboratory.	He does not go into the laboratory.	Does he go into the laboratory?
	She does experiments.	She does not do experiments.	Does she do experiments?

Be careful with plural nouns that are from Greek and Latin origins; make sure you know which form is singular and which is plural. Be sure to use *is* with the singular and *are* with the plural form. For example:

> A *nucleus* is the central region of an atom, made up of protons and neutrons.
>
> The *nuclei* of different elements are different in the numbers of protons and neutrons present.

Past simple

The past simple is used to talk about finished past actions.

Remember the verb *to be* can be used to describe somebody or something and can be followed by adjectives and nouns.

	Affirmative	Negative	Question
I	was	was not	Was I …?
You	were	were not	Were you …?
He	was	was not	Was he …?
She	was	was not	Was she …?
It	was	was not	Was it …?
We	were	were not	Were we …?
They	were	were not	Were they …?

Example sentences:

Affirmative	Negative	Question
I was a student then.	I was not a student then.	Was I a student then?
It was a chemical reaction.	It was not a chemical reaction.	Was it a chemical reaction?
They were metals.	They were not metals.	Were they metals?

Regular past verbs

	Affirmative	Negative	Question
I, you, we, they he, she, it	+ verb +ed	did not + verb	Did + verb to be + verb?

With verbs ending in the letter -*e*, just add *d*.

With verbs ending in a consonant (b, c, d, f, g…) + *y*, change the *y* to an *i* and then add -*ed* when it follows *he, she, it*.

For example:

Vowel + -*y* = *I stay, he stayed.*

Consonant + -*y* = *You try, it tried.*

	Affirmative	Negative	Question
I, you, he, she, it we, they	I observed the changes.	I did not observe the changes.	Did I observe the changes?
	It destroyed the physical structure of the crystals.	It did not destroy the physical structure of the crystals.	Did it destroy the physical structure of the crystals?
	They carried out an experiment.	They did not carry out an experiment.	Did they carry out an experiment?

Irregular past verbs

Some common verbs have irregular past forms. For example: *become, begin, choose, have, know, make, write.*

	Affirmative	Negative	Question
I, you, he, she, it we, they	It became cloudy.	It did not become cloudy.	Did it become cloudy?
	She chose the method.	She did not choose the method.	Did she choose the method?
	They made a solution.	They did not make a solution.	Did they make a solution?

Present passive voice

It is useful to use the passive voice when it is not important what or who (the agent) carrying out the action is, or when the agent is unknown. Using the passive makes the process the most important thing in the sentence. Therefore, the passive voice is often used in scientific writing.

When the verb is active, the subject of the verb is doing the action. You form the active voice with: subject + active verb. For example:

> A reaction *continues* until one of the reactants is all used up.
> The reaction *releases* heat energy, so the system will heat up.
> The external wire and ammeter *complete* the electrolysis circuit.

To form the passive voice, the object of the active sentence becomes the subject of the passive sentence. The passive voice is formed by using: subject + *is/are* + past participle of the verb. For example:

> A reaction *is continued* until one of the reactants is all used up.
>
> Energy from the reaction *is released* as heat, so the system will heat up.
>
> The electrolysis *is completed* by the external wire and ammeter.

The past participle of a regular verb ends with *-ed* and looks the same as the past tense. For example: *behaved, closed, created, performed, slowed.*

The past participle of an irregular verb is the third 'column' when you look at a table of irregular verbs:

Present	Past	Past participle
break	broke	broken
find	found	found
give	gave	given
see	saw	seen
take	took	taken

The zero conditional

The zero conditional is used to talk about facts and things that are generally true. The structure is: *if/when* + present simple + present simple.

> *When* you heat ice, it melts.
>
> *When* an indicator is added to the solution, the colour changes.

The first conditional

The first conditional is used to make predictions and to talk about future actions or events which will probably happen. It is formed by: *If* + present simple + *will* + verb base form/infinitive without *to*. For example:

> *If* the global temperature rises, the glaciers *will melt* rapidly.
>
> *If* sea levels rise significantly, many countries *will* be affected.

Past passive voice

Remember, the passive is used when the person or thing that did the action is unknown, unimportant or not the focus of our interest. We use *by* with the passive if we want to identify who or what did the action.

The past simple passive is formed by using: *was* or *were* + the past participle.

> past active: I *added* the acid to the alkali.
>
> past passive: The acid *was added* to the alkali.

Modal verbs

Modal verbs are different to regular verbs. They do not change for *I, you, we, they, he, she, it,* and they do not use *do/does* in negatives and questions. Modal verbs include *can, could, shall, should, will, would, might, may, must.*

Modal verbs are usually used with other verbs to express ideas such as possibility, necessity, permission, prediction and to make conclusions.

The modal verbs used to express predictions and conclusions are *should, will, could, may* and *might.*

Usage	Modal verb
to show possibility	could may might
to show something possibly will not happen	may not might not
to show something you expect to happen (or not)	will will not
to show that you expect something to happen, if the conditions are correct (or not)	should should not

Example sentences:

> This experiment *could / may / might* go wrong if I don't measure each quantity of substance correctly.
>
> If I don't carry out the experiment carefully, the results *may / might not* be accurate.
>
> Pure water *will* freeze at 0 °C.
>
> When heated aluminium metal comes in contact with chlorine gas, an exothermic reaction *should* happen.

Phrasal verbs

A phrasal verb is a verb followed by a preposition, an adverb or both.

You can add the preposition *up* after some verbs to mean 'completely'. These preposition + verb phrases are called phrasal verbs. Some phrasal verbs are separable, so can have other words in the middle, but inseparable phrasal verbs cannot be separated by other words. The four examples in the table below are all separable.

Phrasal verb	Meaning	Example sentences
split up	fully separate, split into pieces	I am going to *split up* this group. I am going to *split* this group *up*.
break up	similar to 'split up'	A mortar and pestle *breaks up* crystals into a powder. We can *break* crystals *up* into a powder in a mortar and pestle.
clean up	clean everything	We must *clean* everything *up* after the experiment. Everything must be *cleaned up* after the experiment.
use up	all of it has been used, there is nothing left	I have *used up* all of the pages in my book. I have *used* all of the pages in my book *up*.

Nouns

A noun is the name of a person, place, object, process or concept. There are singular and plural nouns.

To name processes taking place, we can use nouns:

> The *evaporation* happened more quickly when the temperature of the water was increased.

Plural nouns

Usually, we change singular nouns into plural nouns by adding -*s* or -*es* to the singular. For example, *flask – flasks, bond – bonds*. If the noun ends in a vowel + -*y*, just add an -*s* to make the plural form. If the noun ends in a consonant + -*y*, the plural form changes the -*y* to -*ies*. For example, *density – densities*.

	Singular	Plural
regular	flask	flasks
	enzyme	enzymes
vowel + -y	alloy	alloys
	key	keys
consonant + -y	theory	theories
	property	properties

Greek- and Latin-based nouns – irregular plurals

Common endings	Singular	Plural
-us → *-i*	nucleus	nuclei
	radius	radii
-a → *-ae*	formula	formulae
-um → *-a*	stratum	strata
	datum	data
-is → *-es*	axis	axes
	analysis	analyses
	hypothesis	hypotheses
-on → *-a*	phenomenon	phenomena
	criterion	criteria

Example sentences:

> The *nucleus* of an atom consists of protons and neutrons..
>
> All *nuclei* of the atoms of an element contain the same number of protons.
>
> H_2O is the chemical *formula* for water. There are many chemical *formulae* to learn.
>
> A *stratum* is a layer of rock in the ground. As I dug deeper in the ground, I saw several separate *strata* of iron ore.
>
> There are two *axes* on a graph. The horizontal *axis* shows temperature.
>
> Read the question *criterion* carefully. Not all *criteria* are the same.

Affect and *effect*

The words *affect* and *effect* are often used in science. It is important to remember the difference between the two.

Affect is usually a verb. For example:

> The presence of a catalyst *affects* the rate of a reaction to increase it.

Effect is usually a noun. For example:

> The *effect* of higher temperatures is that the rate of reaction increases.

Adjectives

Adjectives are words that you can use to describe things, people and places. There are many adjectives in English. Some common examples are *small*, *heavy*, *average*, *precious* and *bright*.

Adjectives go before the thing they are describing (adjective + noun) or after the verb *to be* and sense verbs, for example *seems*, *feels*, *smells*, *looks*, *sounds*. When adjectives modify a pronoun they have to follow the pronoun. For example: *Give me something <u>useful</u>*.

Adjective before noun	Adjective after verb
a *small* particle	The particle is *small*.
heavy rainfall	The rain is *heavy*.
an *average* temperature	The temperature is *average*.
a *precious* stone	The stone is *precious*.
the *bright* lights	The lights are *bright*.

There are many synonyms (words that have the same meaning), for example:

small, tiny, minute (pronounced 'my-NOOT' or 'my-NEWT')

heavy, dense, weighty

average, usual, standard

precious, valuable, rare

Comparative and superlative adjectives

Comparative adjectives are used to compare two nouns. Superlative adjectives are used to compare several things and to express 'the most' or 'the least'.

Comparative adjectives are formed with *-er* and 'more'. Superlative adjectives are formed with *-est* and 'the most'.

Adjectives with one syllable (*big*, *fast*, *small*, ...) add *-er*:

Rule	Adjective	Comparative	Superlative
Most 1-syllable adjectives: add *-er* or *-est*.	tall	taller	the tallest
	long	longer	the longest
	warm	warmer	the warmest
	high	high	the highest
1-syllable adjectives ending in *-e*: add *-r* or *-st*.	large	larger	the largest
	wide	wider	the widest
	safe	safer	the safest
	close	closer	the closest
Adjectives ending consonant–vowel–consonant: double the final consonant then add *-er* or *-est*.	big	bigger	the biggest
	hot	hotter	the hottest
	fit	fitter	the fittest
	thin	thinner	the thinnest

Rule	Adjective	Comparative	Superlative
1-syllable adjectives ending vowel + -y	grey	greyer	the greyest
1- and 2-syllable adjectives ending in a vowel + -w 2-syllable adjectives ending in -le: add -r or -st	few slow narrow simple	fewer slower narrower simpler	the fewest the slowest the narrowest the simplest
1- and 2-syllable adjectives ending consonant + -y: change the y to an i and then add -er or -est.	dry heavy dirty easy icy	drier heavier dirtier easier icier	the driest the heaviest the dirtiest the easiest the iciest
Other 2-syllable adjectives and longer adjectives: use more + adjective or the most + adjective.	active careless colourful important	more active more careless more colourful more important	the most active the most careless the most colourful the most important
Irregular adjectives	good bad far little many	better worse further less more	the best the worst the furthest/farthest the least the most

Use *than* to connect the things being compared:

Reactions at room temperature are slower *than* those at a high temperature.

We tested the acidity levels of lemon juice, tomato juice and coffee. Lemon juice was more acidic *than* tomato juice or coffee.

Adverbs

Adverbs show us how an action is done. Many adverbs of manner are formed by adding *-ly* to the end of adjectives. Adverbs of manner answer the question: 'How?' For example:

The instructions are clear. (process = noun)

He explained the instructions *clearly*. (It shows how the instructions were explained.)

The liquid heated up *quickly*. (It shows how the liquid heated up.)

The balloon burst *loudly*. (It shows how the balloon burst.)

The beaker was *fully* filled. (It shows how the beaker was filled.)

Articles

Indefinite and definite articles *a, an, the*

The indefinite articles *a* and *an* are used to talk about one general person or thing.

The definite article *the* is used to talk about one or more specific person or thing.

The is used when only one of something exists. For example:

> *The* Earth's atmosphere mainly consists of nitrogen and oxygen.
> (There is only one planet Earth.)

The is also used when everybody knows which one we are talking about:

> Look at *the* book.
> (There are many books in school, but you are using one specific book in class.)

The first time something is mentioned, you can use *a* or *an*, but the second time the same thing is mentioned, we now know what is being talked about, so we can use *the*:

> I want to do an experiment. *The* experiment will test the pH of each substance.
> We carried out an experiment. The aim of *the* experiment was to react sodium safely with water.

With phrases: *the* + noun + *of* or *the* + noun + *in*:

> *The* process *of* corrosion is when metals are attacked by other chemical substances.
> *The* molecules *in* a gas are in constant motion.

Note: when making a generalisation, for example about all elements, you can't use *the* because *the* is for specific things only:

> Elements are generally classified as either a metal or nonmetal.

Prefixes

A prefix is a letter or a group of letters added to the beginning of words to change the meaning of the root word. A root word is the basic form of the word, in its shortest form.

Prefix	Meaning	Example
in-	not	*in*soluble – does not dissolve
un-	not	*un*saturated – not saturated
ir-	not	*ir*regular – not regular
iso-	same	*iso*tope – atoms of same element with different mass number
sub-	under / smaller	*sub*merge / *sub*divide
an-	without / lacking	*an*hydrous – without water
de-	process of taking away	*de*hydrate – remove water from

Note that the prefix *ir-* is used before root words that start with the letter *r*.

> Sulfur is *insoluble* in water.
>
> Ethene is an *unsaturated* hydrocarbon as hydrogen can be added to it.
>
> The symbol Au does not match the name of the element gold, which makes it an *irregular* example for the symbol of an element.
>
> *Isotopes* are atoms of the same element that have different numbers of neutrons in their nuclei.
>
> To *submerge* is to keep something under the surface of water.
>
> *Anhydrous* copper(II) sulfate is a solid white powder.
>
> Blue copper(II) sulfate crystals can be *dehydrated* to form a white anhydrous powder.

Prefixes indicating numbers

Prefix	Meaning	Example
mono-	one	carbon monoxide – this molecule contains one oxygen atom
di-, bi-	two	diatomic – a molecule containing only two atoms bisect – to cut in half
tri-	three	sulfur trioxide – this molecule contains three oxygen atoms
tetra-	four	tetrachloride – a chloride containing four atoms of chlorine
pent(a)-	five	pentane – a hydrocarbon molecule with five carbon atoms
hex-	six	hexane – a hydrocarbon containing six carbon atoms
hept-	seven	heptane – a hydrocarbon containing seven carbon atoms
oct-	eight	octane – a hydrocarbon containing eight carbon atoms
non-	nine	nonane – a hydrocarbon containing nine carbon atoms
deci-	one tenth	decimetre – one tenth of a metre
centi-	one hundredth	centimetre – one hundredth of a metre
poly-	many	polymer – a long-chain molecule containing many repeating monomer units

Prefixes indicating the size of a unit

Prefix	Meaning	Example
kilo-	a thousand	kilogram – 1000 grams
milli-	a thousandth	millilitre – 1000th of a litre

General prefixes

Prefix	Meaning	Example
radi-	ray (of light), emission	radiant – sending out light
inter-	between	intermolecular force – the forces between molecules when they are near each other
hydr-, hydro-	water	hydrolysis – splitting a compound by adding water, hydrated – containing water
exo-	out	exothermic – a process resulting in the release of heat
endo-	in	endothermic – a process resulting in the absorption of heat

Suffixes

A suffix is a letter or a number of letters added to the end of a root word. Suffixes can help us to identify if the word is a noun, an adjective, an adverb or a verb. Many verbs in English can be changed into nouns by adding a suffix.

Common suffixes to create nouns from verbs are listed in the table:

Suffix	Word	Example sentence
-ation	ionisation	Ionis*ation* is when an atom gains or loses electrons to become an ion.
-ity	ductility	Ductil*ity* is the capacity to undergo physical stretching without breaking.
-meter	thermometer	A thermo*meter* is a device to measure temperature.
-ment	measurement	We can measure the property of matter and express this measure*ment* as a quantity.
-ent	dependent	The value of a depend*ent* variable depends on the independent variable.

The suffix *-ation* is added to the end of many verbs to create nouns, for example *react – reaction*. If the verb ends in *-e*, change the *-e* to *-ation*. For example:

Verb	Noun
distil	distill*ation*
equate	equa*tion*
condense	condens*ation*
corrode	corros*ion*
diffuse	diffus*ion*
oxidise	oxidat*ion*

Example sentences:

> *Distillation* is a method of separating a solvent from a solution. The solvent *distils* over as it has a lower boiling point.
>
> *Condensation* is when water vapor becomes liquid, for example when water vapour in the air *condenses* into droplets of water.
>
> An example of *oxidation* is that magnesium *oxidises* when it reacts with oxygen to form magnesium oxide.

Some verbs end in *-fy*; in this case you need to change *-y* to *-ication*. For example:

Verb	Noun
acidify	acidi*fication*
classify	classi*fication*
emulsify	emulsi*fication*
intensify	intensi*fication*
solidify	solidi*fication*

Acidification is when something becomes acidic. For example, ocean *acidification* occurs when pollutants *acidify* the water present.

Emulsification occurs when two liquids that normally don't mix are shaken together. You *emulsify* liquids when mixing oil and vinegar in recipes.

Solidification is when a liquid becomes solid. Lava will *solidify* when it cools.

The product of the change is also a noun:

Maya collected the *condensate* in a cooled flask.

Common suffixes to show adjectives are listed in the table:

Suffix	Word	Example sentence
-al	universal	Univers*al* indicator paper shows the pH of a substance.
-able, -ible	flammable	Butane is highly flamm*able*.
-ary	dietary	Some people have special diet*ary* requirements.
-ful	skilful	I am skil*ful* at calculations.
-ic	scientific	I enjoy conducting scientif*ic* investigations.
-ive	cooperative	We must be cooperat*ive* when working in a group.
-less	useless	The broken beaker was use*less*.
-ous	dangerous	Some chemicals are danger*ous*.
-ed	filtered	The filter*ed* water was clean.

Common suffixes to show verbs are *-s*, *-es*, *-ed*, *-ing*. For example:

She *conducts* experiments very well.

We *conducted* the experiment very well.

The temperature of the liquid went up while I was *conducting* the experiment.

Suffixes *-ide* and *-ate*

There are two main systems for naming chemical compounds.

1   Simple binary compounds are compounds containing two elements. Remember, the prefix *bi-* means 'two'. Metals and hydrogen are named first, then the ending of the non-metal's name becomes *-ide*. For example:

magnesium chloride	iron sulfide	potassium oxide

If the compound contains two non-metals, oxygen or the halogen are named second, for example:

carbon dioxide	nitrous oxide	sulfur dioxide

2   Compounds containing two elements (or more) plus oxygen. This includes compound groups such as carbonate, nitrate, etc. The metal is named first. The non-metal is then named and *-ate* is added to indicate the presence of oxygen:

calcium carbonate	potassium iodate	iron sulfate

Exceptions:

• Compounds with historical names, e.g. water, ammonia

• Compounds formed from the reaction of ammonia with acids – the ammonium group is named first, e.g. ammonium bromide

• Metal hydroxides, e.g. sodium hydroxide – these contain two or more elements plus oxygen, but their names end in *-ide*.

Prepositions

There are many prepositions in English. Prepositions are short words which show direction, time, place, location, spatial relationships, or introduce an object. Prepositions usually go before a noun or pronoun.

Prepositions of position

These prepositions refer to things which are not moving or static.

Preposition	Meaning	Example
in	inside an object	The information is *in* the book.
within	inside a set of parameters	The results observed *within* the range of temperature studied show that the reaction rate increases linearly.
		All elements *within* a certain group share similar properties.
between	at, into or across the space separating two objects	Intermolecular space is the space *between* particles of a substance.
		Carbon dioxide molecules consist of a carbon atom *between* two oxygen atoms.
at	the location, the place something is located	The title is *at* the top of the page.
		Silt is *at* the bottom of the river.
		At the end of the chain
on	in contact with the surface	Less dense objects can float *on* water.
		The Periodic Table is *on* the wall.
		The equipment is *on* the table.
under(neath)	directly below something	Carbon, oxygen and copper are classified *under* the heading 'elements'.
		Oxides, chlorides and nitrates are listed *under* 'compounds'.
above	in the space over or higher than an object	Hydrogen is a non-metal, and it is sometimes placed *above* the halogens in the Periodic Table.

Prepositions of motion

These prepositions are related to movement and at least one of the nouns will be moving.

Preposition	Meaning	Example
into	movement towards something or someone	I poured the liquid *into* the beaker.
to	approaching or moving towards a location	Heat transfers from one object *to* another.
from	indicating the place at which a motion or action starts	Frequent collisions slow down the overall rate of diffusion *from* one place to another.
towards	moving in the direction of something	Positively charged ions move *towards* the negatively-charged cathode during electrolysis.
through	moving in one side and out of the other side	In diffusion, the chemical particles move *through* the air and mix with the air particles.
along	moving in a particular direction	The condensed liquid travelled *along* the tube.
over	at a higher level than another object or surface	Dangerous gases can be trapped in the atmosphere *over* a city.

Expressing differences

To show contrast between two or more things, you can use the adjective *different*. *Different* means 'not the same', and can be followed by the prepositions *to* and *from*. The noun *difference* is followed by *between*.

Different to and *different from* have exactly the same meaning, so you can use either.

Noun + *is different to/from* + noun:

> A cation is *different to/from* an anion because a cation moves towards the cathode in electrolysis while an anion moves towards the anode.
>
> A typical hydrogen atom is *different to/from* a hydrogen molecule because it is just a single atom, but a hydrogen molecule contains two hydrogen atoms covalently bonded together.

Difference between has a similar meaning but is formed like this: *the difference between* + noun + noun + *is/are* that…:

> The *differences between* iron and sulfur are that iron is a metal and is attracted to a magnet, but sulfur is a yellow non-metal and is not attracted to a magnet.
>
> The *difference between* salt crystals and sugar crystals is that sugar crystals taste sweet but salt crystals do not.

If you want to show that there are no differences, you can use *same* with *as*:

> Potassium reacts in the *same* way *as* sodium when added to cold water.

Dependent prepositions

Dependent prepositions are prepositions that depend on or must follow a particular verb, noun or adjective. There are no rules to help you with these, so it is good to remember the common examples.

Verb + preposition	Person, object or action	Example sentences
listen to	Name / Pronoun the + who or what	*Listen to* Piotr. *Listen to* her. *Listen to* the teacher. *Listen to* the audio file.
look at	Name / Pronoun the + who or what	*Look at* Siti. *Look at* him. *Look at* the scientist. *Look at* the screen.
depend on	Name / Pronoun the + who or what	It *depends on* you. It *depends on* the results.
consist of	what	Water molecules *consist of* hydrogen and oxygen. Air *consists of* mainly nitrogen and oxygen.
result in	what	Mixing oil and water *results in* an emulsion. Mixing salt and water *results in* a salt solution.
use for	verb + *-ing* (action)	A Bunsen burner is *used for* heating substances up. A microscope is *used for* looking at things in detail.

Connectives

Connectives (or linkers) are words or phrases that act like glue and join two parts of a sentence together. There are many connectives in English, and it is important to choose the right one for each sentence because they work differently and can change the meanings of sentences.

Connectives for addition

To express addition, you can use *as well as*, *in addition to*, *furthermore* and *also*.

For example:

> Sodium is an alkali metal, *as well as* being solid at room temperature.
> Sodium is an alkali metal, *in addition to* being solid at room temperature.
> Alkali metals are very reactive with air and water; *furthermore*, they are relatively soft metals and easily cut.
> Alkali metals are very reactive with air and water; they *also* are relatively soft metals and easily cut.

Connectives for fact, consequence and hypothesis

To express a fact + a consequence, you can use *so*, *because* and *which suggests that*. You form the sentence: fact, *so* + consequence. For example:

Fact	Connective (linker)	Consequence
The reaction between an acid and an alkali is exothermic	so	the temperature of the reaction mixture increases.

or

Consequence	Connective	Fact
The temperature of the reaction mixture increases	because	the reaction between an acid and an alkali is exothermic.

or

Fact	Connective	Hypothesis
The reaction between an acid and an alkali is exothermic	which suggests that	the temperature of the reaction mixture will increase.

Connectives for cause and consequence

To express a cause + a consequence, you can use *because*, *so*, *as*, *therefore* and *consequently*.

Because is used to express the cause and *so, as, therefore* are used to express the consequence. For example:

Connective	Cause	Consequence
As	the reaction between an acid and an alkali is exothermic,	the temperature of the reaction mixture will increase.

or

Consequence	Connective	Cause
The temperature of the reaction mixture will increase	as	the reaction between an acid and an alkali is exothermic.

or

Cause	Connective	Consequence
The reaction between an acid and an alkali is exothermic.	Therefore,	the temperature of the reaction mixture will increase.

or

Cause	Connective	Consequence
The reaction between an acid and an alkali is exothermic.	Consequently,	the temperature of the reaction mixture will increase.

Although you can use *as* at the start of a sentence or in the middle, *therefore* generally goes before the second piece of information.

When you use *as* at the start of a sentence, you need a comma (,) at the end of the phrase.

When you use *Therefore*, you need a comma after it.

Connectives to show purpose and aims

To express purpose and aims, you can use *in order to* and *so that*. *In order to* and *so that* mean the same thing, but different grammar is used after them.

	Connective	Infinitive	
You store alkali metals in oil	in order to	stop	a reaction from happening.

or

Connective	Infinitive		
In order to	stop	a reaction from happening,	store alkali metals in oil.

or

	Connective	Subject	Verb
You store alkali metals in oil	so that	a reaction	does not occur.

or

	Connective	Subject	Verb
You store alkali metals in oil	so that	they	do not react.

Connecting similar things

You can connect two things which are similar by using the word *both*, *both of the* or *both of them*:

> There are many different types of acidic substances. Vinegar and lemon juice are *both* acidic.
>
> Vinegar and lemon juice are common substances; *both of the* liquids are acidic.
>
> Vinegar and lemon juice are common substances; *both of them* are acidic.

Expressing differences – *but, however, although, despite*

You can express the difference between things by using *but*, *however*, *although* and *despite*. Note that *however* is used at the start of the sentence.

* *but* and *however*:

> Acids react with some metals and release hydrogen gas, *but* alkalis do not.
> (Note that you do not need to repeat the action.)
>
> An alkali produces an excess of hydroxide ions when dissolved in water, *but* an acid produces an excess of hydrogen ions.
>
> Many bases are insoluble. *However*, if a base does dissolve in water, we also call it an alkali.
>
> Acids react with some metals and release hydrogen gas. *However*, alkalis do not.

- *although* and *despite*:

  Although and *despite* are used to connect two contrasting ideas or show that one fact makes the other fact surprising. They can be used either at the beginning or in the middle of the sentence.

  Although is followed by a subject and a verb:

  > *Although* I have learned a lot in my chemistry lessons, I need more practice with reactions.
  > I have learned a lot in my chemistry lessons, *although* I need more practice with reactions.

  Despite is followed by a noun or a gerund (*-ing* form of a verb).

  > It gave off heat *despite* the small flame.
  > The reaction didn't occur, *despite* following the instructions carefully.

  It is common to use *despite the fact that*:

  > The experiment didn't work, *despite the fact that* we followed the instructions carefully.

Connecting reason to a deduction – *because, as, so, therefore*

You can use the same connectives as you use for cause and effect to connect the reason why to a deduction. A deduction is the process of reaching a decision or answer by considering the known facts.

When you use these connectives, we often use *must be* to introduce the deduction. This indicates that the deduction is an educated guess:

> *Because | As* sodium floats on water, sodium *must be* less dense than water.
> Sodium floats on water. *Therefore,* sodium *must be* less dense than water.
> Sodium is less dense than water, *so* sodium *must be* able to float on water.

Because is a common connective, but *given that* and *since* can also be used to express the same meaning. They are used at the start or in the middle of the sentence:

> *Given that* sodium is less dense than water, sodium *must be* able to float on water.
> *Since* sodium is less dense than water, sodium *must be* able to float on water.

Another linker you can use in place of *therefore,* is *for this reason,*:

> Sodium floats on water. *For this reason,* sodium *must be* less dense than water.

Chemical calculations

In science, you often need to compare the mass, volume or length of two things. To compare things, you will need to use words and phrases such as *more/less*, *as much as*, *times greater than/less than*.

Calculation	Example sentence
noun + *has two times more mass than* + noun	A sulfur atom *has two times more mass* than an oxygen atom.
noun + *has twice the mass of* + noun	A sulfur atom *has twice the mass of* an oxygen atom.
the mass of + noun + *is X times greater than the mass of* + noun	The mass of a carbon atom *is 12 times greater than the mass of* a hydrogen atom.
noun + *is X times as much as* + noun	The mass of a carbon atom *is 12 times as much as* the mass of a hydrogen atom.
noun + *has half as much mass as* + noun	A carbon atom *has half as much mass as* a magnesium atom.
noun + *has a mass X times less than* + noun	A boron atom *has a mass five times less than* a manganese atom.
noun + *has double the mass of* + noun	A magnesium atom *has double the mass of* a carbon atom.
noun + *is half the mass of* + noun	The mass of a carbon atom *is half that of* a magnesium atom.
noun + *has a third/quarter of the mass of* + noun	A beryllium atom *has a third of the mass of* an aluminium atom.
the mass of + noun + *is a third/quarter of the mass of* + noun	The mass of a beryllium atom *is a third of the mass of* an aluminium atom.
noun + *is X times greater than* + noun	Calcium *is 10 times greater than* helium in atomic mass.

Much and *many* are used to say that there is a large number of something. *Much* is used with uncountable nouns, for example air, water and oil. *Many* is used with countable nouns, for example atoms, cells and substances.

Many		
+	There are *many* different elements.	
−	There are not *many* atoms in a small molecule.	
?	Are there *many* magnetic metals?	

Much	
+	There is *much* pressure in this jar.
−	There isn't *much* oxygen in space.
?	Is there *much* heat energy in a blast furnace?

Note that *much* sounds quite formal in positive sentences, so instead *a lot of* is more commonly used. For example: There is *a lot of* pressure in this jar.

Symbols

When you write a calculation, you can use symbols instead of words. However, when you speak, you need to know how to say these operations in words. There are two ways to do this:

When you read an equation		
Word(s)	Symbol	Examples
plus	+	Twenty *plus* ten per cent equals twenty-two.
minus	−	A hundred *minus* twenty-five per cent is seventy-five.
times	×	Twenty *times* five equals a hundred.
divided by, over, into	÷	Ten *divided by* two equals five. Ten *over* two equals five. Two *into* ten equals five.
equals is	=	Ten times five *equals* fifty. Ten times five *is* fifty.

When you read a sentence		
Word(s)	Symbol	Examples
add	+	*Add* both numbers together. Calculate by *adding* both numbers together.
subtract	−	If you *subtract* twenty from sixty you get forty.
multiply by	×	*Multiply* fifty *by* five.
divide by	÷	*Divide* the result *by* two.
equals	=	Ten divided by two *equals* five.

> Chapter 1
States of matter

IN THIS CHAPTER YOU WILL:

Science skills:

- describe the key properties of the physical states of matter and the changes that take place between them

- understand the kinetic particle theory of matter and the nature of diffusion and dissolving.

English skills:

- meet and practise the verbs involved in describing changes of physical state, and the nouns resulting from those verbs

- develop the ability to construct sentences linking facts and their consequences.

Exercise 1.1 The three states of matter

IN THIS EXERCISE YOU WILL:

Science skills:

- describe the key properties of the different physical states of matter and the changes of state brought about by changing temperature.

English skills:

- look at the use of verbs and nouns when describing chemical processes.

KEY WORDS

boiling: the process of change from liquid to gas at the boiling point of the substance; a condition under which gas bubbles are able to form within a liquid – gas molecules escape from the body of a liquid, not just from its surface

evaporation: a process occurring at the surface of a liquid, involving the change of state from a liquid into a vapour at a temperature below the boiling point

fluid: a gas or a liquid; they are able to flow

matter: anything that occupies space and has mass

1   a   The table below shows how the particles are arranged in a solid, liquid and gas. Complete the table using information in Figure 1.1 and your own knowledge.

a 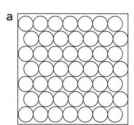   b 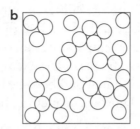   c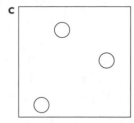

Figure 1.1: The arrangement of particles in a: a solid, b: a liquid and c: a gas.

Physical state	Volume	Density	Shape	Fluidity
solid	has a fixed volume	....	has a definite shape	does not flow
liquid	has a fixed volume	moderate to high	does not have a .... – takes the shape of the container	generally ....
gas	does not have a .... – expands to fill the container and can be compressed	....	does not have a definite shape – takes the shape of the container	flows easily

b   Complete the following sentences i–v using the words below. Each word should be used only once. Note that the sentences express comparisons.

compressed   expands   fixed   fluid   higher

lower   more   pressure

i   Most solid substances have a .... density than their liquid or gas form.

ii   The density of a gas is .... than that of the liquid state.

iii   The volumes of a solid and a liquid are ...., but a gas .... to fill the container it is in.

iv   Both gases and liquids are .... states. A gas is .... **fluid** than a liquid.

v   Solids and liquids have a fixed volume which is not changed by increasing the pressure. However, gases can be .... by increased ....

LANGUAGE TIP

You can compare things using comparative adjectives with *than*. Short adjectives become comparative when you add *-er*; longer adjectives become comparative by adding *more* before them. (See Chapter 8.)

2 a Read the following passage, then complete the labels in the diagram.

All chemical substances can exist in three different physical states depending on the conditions. These different states of **matter** are solid, liquid and gas. Changing the temperature can change the state in which the substance exists. Increasing the temperature will eventually cause most solids to melt and become liquid. The temperature at which a solid melts is its melting point.

If a liquid is left alone, it will slowly evaporate. It becomes a vapour or gas. **Evaporation** can happen at any temperature, but if the temperature is increased enough, it will reach a point where the liquid boils. Bubbles of gas form in the liquid and this temperature is the **boiling** point. Some substances evaporate and boil very easily. They are volatile.

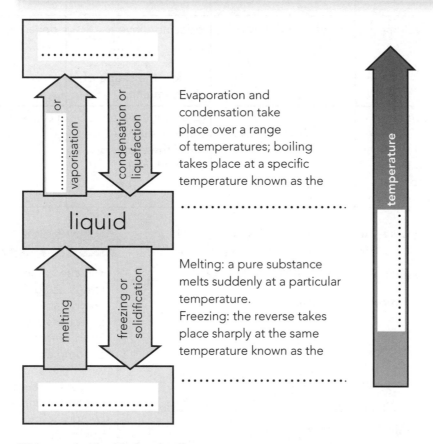

b Write a suitable title for the diagram.

....

LANGUAGE FOCUS

When you describe the action of a substance changing state, or of an agent (e.g. a person) carrying out an action, you use a verb. For example, the verb *to filter*:

The salt crystals were <u>filtered</u> from the solution using filter paper.

When you look for a verb in a dictionary, you will often find it with *to* before it, but you frequently do not need to use the *to*.

The names of the processes taking place are nouns:

Maya carried out the <u>filtration</u> using filter paper and a funnel.

Note that most nouns describing processes end in *-ation*. If the verb ends in *-e*, change the *-e* to *-ation*. However, with some verbs, particularly verbs ending in *-fy* (e.g. solidify), you need to change the *-y* to *-ication*.

The product of the change is also a noun:

Maya collected the <u>filtrate</u> in a conical flask.

3   Complete the table with the correct forms of the words.

Verb	Noun – name of process	Noun – product of process
to condense	....	....
to	evaporation	vapour
to	....	crystals
to precipitate	....	precipitate
to	solidification	solid

Exercise 1.2 Explaining physical processes

IN THIS EXERCISE YOU WILL:

Science skills:

*   investigate changes of state based on the key ideas of scientific observation, explanation and definition.

English skills:

*   use linkers *so*, *because* and *which suggests that* to link scientific facts with consequences and hypotheses.

LANGUAGE FOCUS

Compare these sentences:

1 *The melting point of ice is 0 °C, <u>so</u> it becomes liquid at higher temperatures.*

2 *Ice becomes liquid at temperatures higher than 0 °C <u>because</u> it is above its melting point.*

The melting point of ice is 0 °C = a fact.

It becomes liquid at higher temperatures = a consequence, result or logical conclusion.

If the fact is before the consequence, use *so*.

If the consequence is before the fact, use *because*.

Sometimes a fact gives us an idea for a new theoretical explanation, or hypothesis. If so, we can link the fact and the hypothesis using *which suggests that*:

Fact	Hypothesis

Liquids are fluid, <u>which suggests that</u> the particles in liquids can move around.

---

4 The following sentences **a–g** consist of two parts. For each sentence, decide which part expresses the fact and which part expresses the consequence, then complete each sentence using *because*, *so* or *which suggests that*. Here is an example to help you:

Iron is denser than water, <u>so</u> a block of iron sinks when placed on the surface of water.

a Ice floats on water, ..., unusually, liquid water is denser than solid water (ice).

b Ethanol is more volatile than water, ... it will evaporate more quickly than water at the same temperature.

c A gas spreads out to fill its container .... the particles of a gas can move around freely.

d A liquid can be poured from one beaker to another .... a liquid is fluid and can flow from one place to another.

e A gas can be compressed when pressure is applied, ... there is space between the particles in a gas.

5   The following questions discuss different terms used to describe changes of state.

a   Match the sentence halves in the following grid by drawing lines to connect the correct halves. The first one has been done for you.

1	Freezing is the process…		A	… *that* can flow from one place to another.
2	Fluids are substances…		B	… *which* a solid turns into a liquid.
3	The melting point is the temperature at…		C	… *that* turns a liquid into a gas.
4	Boiling is a process…		D	… *that* turns a liquid into a solid.

LANGUAGE TIP

Sentences with important terms and their definitions, like the sentences in Exercise 5a, are useful to learn 'by heart'. Make a note of this type of sentence in your notebook and look at them from time to time.

b   Put the words below the terms **i–iv** in the correct order to give the definition of the term. The first one has been done for you.

i   **boiling point**

which temperature the gas bubbles of at formed are a liquid throughout boils and liquid the. gas liquid into the turns a.

The temperature at which bubbles of gas are formed throughout a liquid and the liquid boils. The liquid turns into a gas.

ii   **volatile**

a word describe to used liquid boiling point that a has and easily low a evaporates.

....

....

iii   **freezing**

reverse which the is process the melting of can solidification called also be and.

....

....

iv   **evaporation**

turns a into liquid the which gas below a point boiling its process.

....

....

Exercise 1.3 The kinetic particle theory

IN THIS EXERCISE YOU WILL:

Science skills:

- investigate the nature of the different states and the changes between them in terms of how the particles present are organised.

English skills:

- complete a short paragraph to describe the different states and the movement of the particles in them.

KEY WORDS

kinetic particle theory: a theory which accounts for the bulk properties of the different states of matter in terms of the movement of particles (atoms or molecules) – the theory explains what happens during changes in physical state

6   The **kinetic particle theory** describes the organisation and movement of particles in the three states of matter (see Figure 1.2).

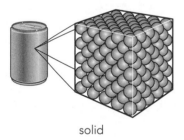
solid

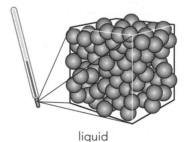
liquid

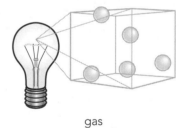
gas

Figure 1.2: Organisation of particles in the three states of matter.

a   Circle the correct options to complete this description of a gas.

The particles in a gas are far apart in **fixed / random** positions.
Their arrangement is totally **regular / irregular**. The particles are **able / unable** to move around freely; they **can / can't** collide, or bounce off each other.

b   Complete the following description of a liquid. Use the description of a gas in part **a** as a model.

The particles in a liquid are packed closely together. Their arrangement is

.... The particles are .... to move around

freely, though they can often .... with each other.

LANGUAGE TIP

Prefixes can help you understand words. For example, words with un- (*unable*, *unstable*) or ir- (*irregular*, *irrelevant*) mean 'not' (*not able, not stable, not regular, not relevant*).

7   **a**   Circle the correct words in paragraphs **i** and **ii** to complete descriptions of
what happens to the movement of the particles as a solid or a liquid is heated.

   i   As a solid is heated the particles **rotate / vibrate** more **strongly / weakly**.
At the **condensation point / melting point** the particles have enough
energy / power to break the forces holding them in one place. Now they
can **move / step** past each other, and so we see that the solid
freezes / melts and turns to **liquid / vapour**.

   ii   As the **volume / temperature** rises the particles in a liquid **lose / gain**
more energy and move around **faster / slower**. Some particles can escape
from the surface; this is **evaporation / condensation**. The temperature
increases until the **boiling point / evaporation point** is reached. At this
point the particles have enough energy to break the forces holding the
liquid together. Gas **bubbles / drops** form in the liquid and the liquid
steams / boils.

   b   Use the phrases given to complete the following paragraph describing how
particles change their movement and organisation when a liquid freezes.

   turns into a solid   forces between particles   lose energy

   move around more slowly   fixed positions   freezing point

   As the liquid cools, the particles .... and

   .... The ....

   become stronger. At the ...., the particles

   become held in ...., and so the liquid freezes

   and ....

Exercise 1.4 Diffusion and dissolving

IN THIS EXERCISE YOU WILL:

Science skills:

- describe how the movement of particles in a liquid or gas results in the
processes of diffusion and dissolving.

English skills:

- become more familiar with the specific words used to describe diffusion
and dissolving.

KEY WORDS

diffusion: the process by which different fluids mix as a result of the random
motions of their particles

dissolving: a process that produces a solution of a solid or gas in a liquid,
e.g. when sugar dissolves in water

8   **Diffusion** allows substances to spread and mix; the particles move to fill all the available volume (see Figure 1.3). It is a key part of the process of **dissolving**.

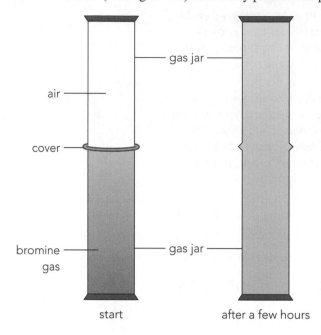

gas jar

air

cover

bromine gas — gas jar

Bromine vapour spreads to fill the whole container, including the top gas jar, when the cover is removed. The colour of the vapour is lighter.

start   after a few hours

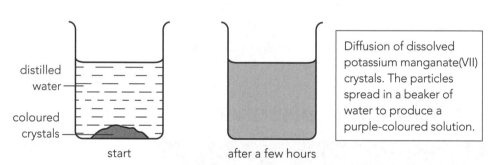

distilled water

coloured crystals

Diffusion of dissolved potassium manganate(VII) crystals. The particles spread in a beaker of water to produce a purple-coloured solution.

start   after a few hours

Figure 1.3: Diffusion of a gas and in a liquid.

Complete the following bullet points about diffusion.

Diffusion:

•   is the process occurring when ....

•   is a random process that can only take place in ....

•   is much faster in ....

•   is faster at higher ....

9 **a** Here are ten important words used in describing how substances dissolve.

concentrated   dilute   dissolved   insoluble   saturated

soluble   solute   solution   solvent   undissolved

Find three pairs of words with opposite meanings.

dilute ....   c ....

....

....

b Using the four words you did not use in part **a**, complete the following sentences.

i A .... is made up of a .... dissolved in

a ....

ii When no more .... can be dissolved at a particular

temperature, the .... is said to be ....

> Chapter 2
Atomic structure

IN THIS CHAPTER YOU WILL:

Science skills:

- investigate atomic structure and the meaning of the terms atomic number, mass number and isotopes

- describe the relationship between the electronic configuration of an atom and the Periodic Table.

English skills:

- learn how to respond to the command word *explain*

- look at how prefixes define and modify words.

Exercise 2.1 Atoms and molecules: words and meanings

IN THIS EXERCISE YOU WILL:

Science skills:

- become familiar with the fact that substances can exist as elements, compounds and mixtures, and are made up of small particles (atoms or molecules).

English skills:

- develop confidence using words that are important in discussing the nature of substances.

1   a   Find five important terms in the following word string and write them on the lines given. They relate to the different types of substance that exist and to the particles they consist of. The first has been done for you.

mixturemoleculeelementatomcompound

~~mixture~~   ....

b The table contains definitions of the terms in part **a**. Complete the table with the correct words. The first one has been done for you.

Term	Definition
........mixture........	two or more chemical substances physically mixed together but not chemically combined
....	a chemical substance made from two or more elements chemically bonded together
....	a particle made up of more than one atom chemically bonded together
....	a chemical 'building block' of all matter that cannot be broken down into simpler substances
....	the smallest particle of an element that can take part in a chemical reaction

c The diagrams show the arrangement of particles in four gases (**A–D**). Label the gases by writing one of *element*, *mixture* or *compound* under each diagram. Use the information in the table to help you.

A	B	C	D

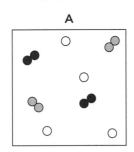
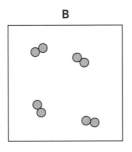
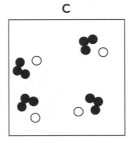
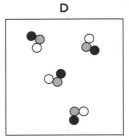

A = ...mixture.......   B = ...   C = ...   D = ...

Exercise 2.2 Atomic structure

IN THIS EXERCISE YOU WILL:

Science skills:

• understand that atoms are made up of protons, neutrons and electrons.

English skills:

• practise how to write an explanation as an answer to a specific question.

KEY WORDS

isotopes: atoms of the same element which have the same proton number but a different nucleon number; they have different numbers of neutrons in their nuclei; some isotopes are radioactive because their nuclei are unstable (radioisotopes)

nucleus: (of an atom) the central region of an atom that is made up of the protons and neutrons of the atom; the electrons orbit around the nucleus in different 'shells' or 'energy levels'

2   Use the diagram below to answer the questions. Note that all atoms are electrically neutral because they have equal numbers of protons and electrons.

   a   On the diagram, label the **nucleus**, a proton and an electron.

   b   Particles that are found in the nucleus are known as nucleons. Which two particles are nucleons? How many nucleons are there in a lithium atom?

   ....

   ....

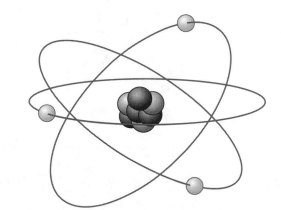

LANGUAGE TIP

In chemistry, you often add *all* before a noun to emphasise that you mean 'every single one'.

Atoms have nuclei. →
All atoms have nuclei.

Gases are fluids. →
All gases are fluids.

LANGUAGE FOCUS

The word *explain* is an important command word. *Explain* means that, as well as describing what happens in a process, you must say why/how it happens. Useful expressions to help you explain a process are:

This is because…   *That's why…*   *The reason for this is…*   *… and so…*

For example:

<u>*Explain*</u> *why it takes longer to cook rice at the top of a high mountain.*

<u>*The reason for this is*</u> *that water boils at a lower temperature at high altitude and so cooler water means a longer cooking time.*

c   Explain this statement by completing the sentence below.

The electrical charge on the nucleus is positive because ....

....

....

d   An atom can accept or lose electrons to become a charged ion. What must happen for an atom to become positively charged? Explain your answer.

....

....

....

e   The electrons in an atom orbit the nucleus in different electron shells (energy levels). Each shell can only contain a certain number of electrons. Use the two diagrams in Figure 2.1 to answer the question that follows.

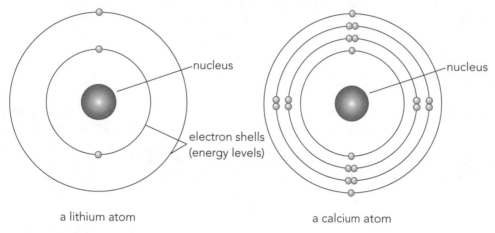

a lithium atom   a calcium atom

Figure 2.1: The electronic configuration of atoms of lithium and calcium.

What do you think is the maximum number of electrons that can be present in the first and second shells of any atom?

first electron shell = ...

second electron shell = ...

3 The composition of any atom is described by two numbers: its proton (or atomic) number and its mass (or nucleon) number. For any atom, these two numbers can be used with the symbol for the element to define the composition of a particular atom. Figure 2.2 shows this form of notation for helium.

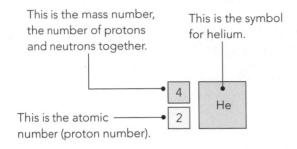

This is the mass number, the number of protons and neutrons together.

This is the symbol for helium.

This is the atomic number (proton number).

Figure 2.2: The atomic notation for helium.

Use the Periodic Table to find out the values of x and y to complete the atomic notation for phosphorus.

x = the mass (or nucleon) number = ...

y = the proton (or atomic) number = ...

$$_y^x\mathrm{P}$$

4 Match the important terms **1–6** in the table with their definitions **A–F**. Write your answers in the grid below the table. The first example has been done for you.

Term		Definition	
1	**isotopes**	A	a negatively charged particle found orbiting the nucleus in an atom
2	electron shell (energy level)	B	the central structure of an atom, usually containing protons and neutrons
3	the nucleus of an atom	C	a positively charged particle found in the nucleus of all atoms
4	electron	D	a particle found in the nucleus of atoms that has the same mass as a proton but no charge
5	proton	E	one of the defined orbits around the nucleus of an atom where electrons can be found
6	neutron	F	atoms of the same element that have different numbers of neutrons in their nuclei

1	2	3	4	5	6
F					

LANGUAGE TIP

Throughout your chemistry course, think about how chemical symbols, atomic notation, molecular formulae, chemical equations, etc., can be considered as the 'language of chemistry'.

Exercise 2.3 The Periodic Table and atomic structure

IN THIS EXERCISE YOU WILL:

Science skills:

- consider how the structure of an atom relates to the position of an element in the Periodic Table.

English skills:

- construct a paragraph by putting ideas in a logical order to explain a concept.

KEY WORDS

electronic configuration: a shorthand method of describing the arrangement of electrons within the electron shells (or energy levels) of an atom; also referred to as electronic structure

5   One important feature in determining the position of elements within the Periodic Table is their **electronic configuration** (see Figure 2.3).

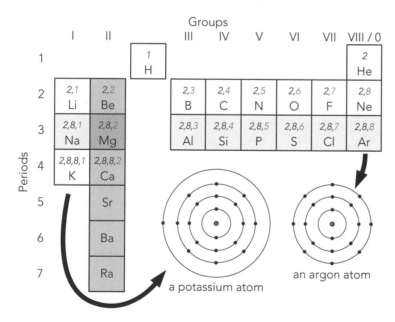

Figure 2.3: The Periodic Table and electronic configuration.

Put the following sentences, or parts of sentences, into the correct order to complete the paragraph about the Periodic Table. (The starting and final sentences of the paragraph have been provided for you.)

a   in the table are called periods. The period ...

b   the known chemical elements are listed in the Periodic Table. In ...

c   that an element is in shows how many shells (energy levels) have electrons in them in an atom of that element. The atoms ...

d   the table the elements are arranged in order of increasing proton number. The proton ...

e   means that the arrangement of atoms in the table is related to the arrangement of electrons in the atoms of the elements. The rows ...

f   number of an element is also the number of electrons in an atom of that element. This ...

g   of the elements in the same column (group) of the table all have the same number of electrons in their outer shell.

All materials are made up from the different chemical elements.

All of ....

....

....

....

....

....

....

....

....

....

....

....

....

....

This finding explains why elements in the same group have similar properties.

Exercise 2.4 Naming chemical substances

IN THIS EXERCISE YOU WILL:

Science skills:

- learn the relationship between the names of certain substances and their chemical formulae.

English skills:

- look at the meaning of numerical prefixes and prefixes that change the meaning of a word.

LANGUAGE FOCUS

A prefix is a group of letters added to the beginning of a word that supports meaning or makes a new word. Many prefixes in English come from Greek or Latin, and it is very useful to know what they mean as they are often used in scientific work. Some of the words used earlier in this book contained important prefixes. Others will be referred to in later exercises.

Some prefixes indicate the number of parts that make up an object or structure:

A _tricycle has three wheels. (tri-_ = three)

A _polygon has many sides. (poly-_ = many)

Other prefixes show the size of a scientific unit. For example, _centi-_ and _deci-_ are particularly important. _Centi-_ indicates 100 and _deci-_ means 10, so you know there are 100 _centi_metres or 10 _deci_metres in a metre. There are 1000 grams in a _kilo_gram, but there are 1000 _milli_grams in a gram.

Some prefixes add extra meaning to the words they are attached to, and can help you understand words around them, too.

When you meet new prefixes, try to work out what they mean; that will help you understand the next word you meet with the same prefix.

LANGUAGE TIP

Look out for frequent 'science' verbs such as _provide_ (= give), _perform_ (= do or carry out) and _place_ (= put), and make a list of them. For example:

Rain provides the trees with water. (= Rain gives the trees water.)

He placed the sample in the dish. (= He put the sample in the dish.)

6   Prefixes are commonly used in the naming of chemical substances to show how many atoms of one kind are present in a molecule. The oxygen in the air is made up of two oxygen atoms chemically bonded together. Technically it could be called di-oxygen. There is another gas in the upper atmosphere whose molecules are made up of three oxygen atoms. It is commonly called ozone, but what would its technical name be? Complete the label in the space provided.

Oxygen or _di-oxygen_

Ozone or ....

7   The names for compounds also use prefixes. Figure 2.4 shows the structure of carbon dioxide.

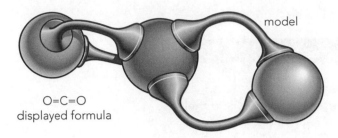

O=C=O
displayed formula

Figure 2.4: The structure of carbon dioxide.

a   How many bonds are made by the atoms in carbon dioxide?

The carbon atom (C) makes .... bonds

Each oxygen (O) atom makes .... bonds

b   The formula of nitrogen monoxide is NO. How many bonds is nitrogen

making in nitrogen monoxide? ....

c   i   Complete the table, which lists several prefixes related to numbers.
        The first line has been completed for you.

Prefix	Meaning of the prefix	Example	Explanation of example
mon(o)-	one of something	carbon monoxide	the molecule contains one oxygen atom
di- or bi-		diatomic	
tri-		sulfur trioxide	
tetra-		tetrachloromethane	
pent(a)-		phosphorus pentoxide	

ii Complete the names of the following chemical compounds by writing in the correct prefix for the number of atoms of oxygen present in the molecule:

NO_2 nitrogen ....oxide

V_2O_5 vanadium ....oxide

P_2O_3 phosphorus ....oxide

d Complete this table, which lists some general examples of prefixes. The first line has been completed for you.

Prefix	Meaning of the prefix	Example	Explanation of example
non-	not having a particular nature or property	non-metal	an element that is not a metal
un-	....	unstable	a substance that breaks down very easily
in-	not having a particular nature or property	....	a substance that is not soluble (does not dissolve)
ir-	not having a particular nature or property	....	having an arrangement that is not organised
sub-	under or smaller than	subatomic particles	....
iso-	same	....	atoms of the same element with different nucleon numbers

Note that the term subatomic particles is useful and widely used to describe protons, neutrons and electrons but is not required knowledge.

LANGUAGE TIP

The prefix *iso-*, meaning 'the same as', is used frequently in science, e.g. *iso*mers = same molecular formula but different structures; *iso*therm = same temperature and *iso*bar = same pressure.

> Chapter 3
Chemical bonding

IN THIS CHAPTER YOU WILL:

Science skills:

- investigate the formation of ions and the nature of ionic compounds

- describe how atoms form molecules by covalent bonding, and the nature of simple molecular and giant molecular structures.

English skills:

- look at how prepositions are used to show the relationship between different things and use linking words to contrast different ideas

- use the present simple to communicate facts that are always true.

Exercise 3.1 Forming chemical bonds

IN THIS EXERCISE YOU WILL:

Science skills:

- describe the basic ideas behind the two major types of bonding in compounds: ionic bonding and covalent bonding.

English skills:

- use prepositions of position and of motion when describing chemical bonding.

KEY WORDS

covalent bonding: chemical bonding formed by the sharing of one or more pairs of electrons between two atoms

ionic bonding: a strong electrostatic force of attraction between oppositely charged ions

molecule: a group of atoms held together by covalent bonds

Prepositions are words that help show the relationship between different things. That relationship is often related to space (*within* the molecule, *to* the cathode) and can express position or motion.

Prepositions of position include *in, within, between, at, on, under(neath)* and *above.* The objects referred to will be static, not moving.

Lithium is __at__ the top of the alkali group of metals __in__ the Periodic Table.

Sodium and potassium are __under__ lithium __in__ Group I.

Covalent bonds are forces __within__ the molecule holding it together.

Prepositions of motion include *into, to, from, towards, through, along* and *over.* At least one of the objects in the sentence will be moving.

The filtrate passes __through__ the filter paper during filtration.

Electrons transfer __from__ the metal to the non-metal to form ionic bonds.

Prepositions always have a noun (*wire, glass, layers*), a pronoun (*it, them, these, which*) or an *-ing* form after them. You will meet prepositions with *-ing* and with *which* in Chapter 21.

1   Complete the following passages, which describe how chemical bonds are formed in **ionic bonding** and **covalent bonding**. Use the words below. You may need some of the words more than once.

between   forces   from   in   lose   metal   non-metals

opposite   positive   sharing   to   transfer   two

Ionic bonding involves the .... of electrons .... one type of atom .... another. It takes place when a compound is formed between a .... and a non-metal. Metal atoms .... electrons to become .... ions, while non-metal atoms accept electrons to become negative ions. Electrostatic .... of attraction .... ions of .... charge hold the structure together.

Covalent bonding involves the .... of electrons .... the outer shells (energy levels) of the atoms being joined. This type of bonding is present .... **molecules** that contain only .... A single covalent bond is made of .... shared electrons.

2   Diagrams are important for describing the different types of bonding.
    Complete the descriptions below the following diagram, which shows both ionic
    and covalent bonding.

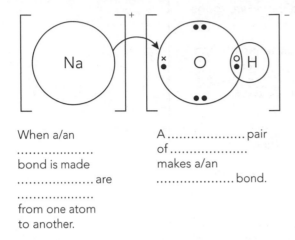

When a/an
....
bond is made
.... are
....
from one atom
to another.

A .... pair
of ....
makes a/an
.... bond.

3   Figure 3.1 shows the covalent bonding in oxygen and carbon dioxide molecules.
    Both have multiple bonds in their molecules.

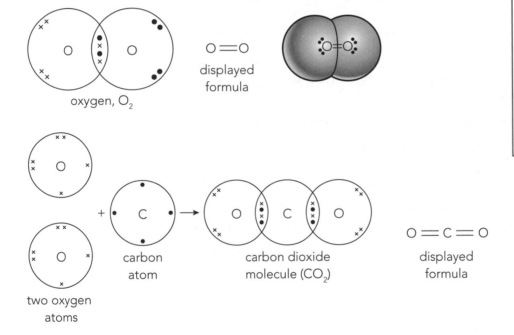

Figure 3.1: The bonding in two gases in the atmosphere.

> ### LANGUAGE TIP
>
> *Single*, *double* and *triple* in front of a noun (a thing) refer to number. They tell you how many identical or connected similar things there are: *single* = one, *double* = two, *triple* = three.

Answer the following questions with a short, complete sentence and include a preposition. Then <u>underline</u> your prepositions.

a How many covalent bonds are there between the atoms in an oxygen molecule?

....

b What word describes the bonds in oxygen and carbon dioxide?

....

c All of the atoms in the two molecules have a share in the same number of electrons in their outer shell. How many electrons is that?

....

....

Exercise 3.2 Ionic compounds

IN THIS EXERCISE YOU WILL:

Science skills:

* describe ionic bonding as the type of bonding found in compounds that contain metals.

English skills:

* use key words and the present simple to talk about ionic bonding.

KEY WORD

ions: charged particles made from an atom, or group of atoms (compound ions), by the loss or gain of electrons

LANGUAGE FOCUS

To talk about facts and things that are always true, use verbs in the present simple. The present simple is easy to form and most verbs are regular.

1 Affirmative (+): for *I, you, we, they* or plural nouns (*diamonds, anions, scientists*), use the basic verb after your subject:

Atoms <u>contain</u> protons, neutrons and electrons.

Anions <u>move</u> to the anode during electrolysis.

Reactions <u>finish</u> when one of the reactants is used up.

CONTINUED

For *it, she, he* or a singular noun (*silica, science, atom*), use the basic verb and add *-s* (most verbs) or *-es* (verbs that end in *sh, ch, s, z* or *o*):

A molecule <u>contains</u> at least two atoms joined together by covalent bonds.

He <u>moves</u> quickly when he is late for a class.

The class <u>finishes</u> after an hour.

2   Negative (–): for *I, you, we, they* or plural nouns, use *do not* + basic verb:

They <u>do not</u> <u>contain</u> atoms or molecules.

Anions <u>do not</u> <u>move</u> to the cathode during electrolysis.

For *it, she, he* or a singular noun, use *does not* + the basic verb:

A molecule <u>does not</u> <u>contain</u> only one single atom.

He <u>does not</u> <u>move</u> quickly even when he is late for a class.

Note: *be* and *have* are irregular.

Be	Positive	Negative
I	am	am not
you/we/they/ scientists/ atoms	are	are not, aren't

Have	Positive	Negative
I/you/we/they/ scientists/ atoms	have	do not have
it/she/he/ electricity/ the scientist	has	does not have

Are not and *is not* are scientific. *Aren't* and *isn't* are only for use in conversation.

4   Sodium chloride (common salt) is an ionic compound. Figure 3.2 shows the transfer of electrons from a sodium atom to a chlorine atom to form **ions**. Each sodium atom donates an electron to a chlorine atom.

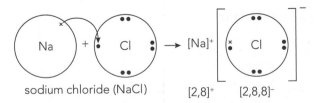

sodium chloride (NaCl) $[2,8]^+$ $[2,8,8]^-$

Figure 3.2: The ionic bonding in sodium chloride.

Circle the correct options in the following statements. Then complete the statements using your own words, to say something about ions.

a Atoms **are / are not** made up of protons, neutrons and electrons.
Any atom **contains / contain** an equal number of protons and electrons.
They **are / are not** neutral.

Ions are atoms, or groups of atoms, that have gained or .... electrons.

They can be positively or .... charged.

b A sodium atom **consist / consists** of 11 protons and 11 electrons.
It **is / is not** neutral.

A sodium ion is a sodium atom that has lost an electron. It has 11 protons

and only 10 ....

Therefore, a sodium ion has a single .... charge.

c Chlorine atoms **are / are not** neutral. They **consist / consists** of 17 protons and 17 electrons.

A chloride ion is a chlorine atom that has accepted an extra electron.

It has 17 .... and .... electrons.

Therefore, a chloride ion has a single .... charge. A chloride ion **is /**

is not an anion and **moves / does not move** to the anode in electrolysis.

5 Sodium and chloride ions have opposite electrical charges. Therefore, they are attracted to each other by electrostatic forces, which are strong. They form a regular arrangement of positive and negative ions (see Figure 3.3). The ions are arranged in an alternating structure (lattice) in all directions.

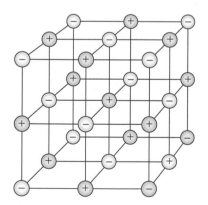

Figure 3.3: An ionic lattice structure.

> ### LANGUAGE TIP
>
> Positive ions (e.g. Na^+, Mg^{2+}) are also known as _cations_ because they move to the _cathode_ in electrolysis. Negative ions (e.g. Cl^-, OH^-) are also known as _anions_ because they move to the _anode_ in electrolysis.

Circle the correct form of the verb to complete the statements. Use information from the text and Figure 3.3 to help.

a State what type of forces hold an ionic crystal lattice together.

Strong .... forces **holds / hold** the ionic lattice together.

b Describe how the sodium ions and chloride ions are arranged in sodium chloride.

The ions **form / forms** a .... arrangement of positive and negative ions.

c Explain why sodium chloride has a relatively high melting point.

The electrostatic forces of .... between the ions **are not / are**

strong and **require / requires** a large amount of energy to break them.

d How many chloride ions surround each sodium ion?

.... chloride ions **surrounds / surround** each sodium ion.

Exercise 3.3 Simple covalent compounds

IN THIS EXERCISE YOU WILL:

Science skills:

- describe the nature of covalent bonds in simple molecular elements and compounds.

English skills:

- become familiar with the language you need to talk about simple molecules and covalent bonding.

6 Figure 3.4 shows the covalent bonding in methane.

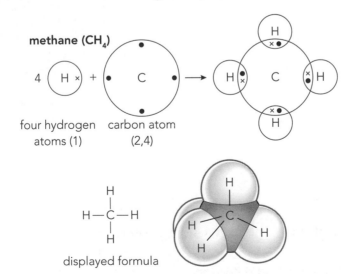

Figure 3.4: The covalent bonding in methane.

Reorder the letters in brackets and complete the following passage with the words. The first has been done for you.

A (eleclomu) ...molecule... of methane consists of one atom of carbon bonded to four hydrogen atoms. The atoms (ahres) .... electrons from their outer shells to make the bonds. The outer shells (povlare) .... Each hydrogen atom shares one of the four outer electrons of the carbon atom.

The carbon atom becomes the (ntcree) .... of the methane molecule.

A covalent single bond is made up of two electrons. It can be represented as a (genlis) .... line in a displayed formula.

In total, the carbon atom has a share of (tgeih) .... electrons in its outer shell. This is a particularly (eblast) .... arrangement of electrons.

It is similar to the electronic configuration of the nearest (obeln) .... gas in the Periodic Table.

LANGUAGE FOCUS

Some words or phrases always work with a particular preposition. It is not always clear why the preposition is correct – it is simply a characteristic of that word. This means it is important to try to learn these types of words or phrases together with their preposition, and to note memorable example sentences to help you learn and practise them.

Here are a few words that work with of and between:

Of: a group/pair of, a molecule of, (be) made up of, consist of, a maximum/ minimum of, an average of, a pair of, a charge of

Between: shared between, formed between, bond between (or bond with), vary between

7   Complete the following sentences using the correct preposition.

between   in   of   throughout

to   towards   with   within

a   In covalent bonding, atoms share electrons .... other atoms to make molecules. In ionic bonding, metal atoms donate outer electrons .... non-metal atoms to make the bond.

b   Atoms share their outer electrons to make the covalent bonds .... a molecule.

c   An oxygen atom can hold a maximum .... eight electrons .... its outer shell when it makes bonds.

d   In making a bond, atoms are transferring or sharing electrons to move
.... a more stable electronic configuration.

e   Covalent compounds are formed .... non-metal elements.

f   Diamond is very hard because it has strong covalent bonds ....
the whole structure.

g   While the forces .... the structures of simple molecules are
strong covalent bonds, the intermolecular forces .... molecules
are generally weak.

Exercise 3.4 Diamond and graphite

IN THIS EXERCISE YOU WILL:

Science skills:

• compare the structures of diamond and graphite, and their properties.

English skills:

• practise the language you need to contrast two different things and look at how to link ideas in a piece of text.

KEY WORDS

giant covalent structures: a substance where large numbers of atoms are held together by covalent bonds forming a strong lattice structure

8   Read the following text, then complete the statements **a–j** using the words in italics.

Covalent bonding can also produce **giant covalent structures**. Examples of these are diamond and graphite, which are two very different forms of the same element, carbon (see Figure 3.5).

Diamond is colourless and *transparent*. In diamond, the carbon atoms are arranged *tetrahedrally*. The atoms form a large, *three-dimensional* structure. The structure is very strong, which makes diamond very hard.

Graphite is grey and *shiny* in *appearance*. It has a *layered* structure. In each *two-dimensional* layer, the carbon atoms are arranged *hexagonally*. The layers lie on top of each other; they can move across each other easily, which means graphite is *slippery*. Graphite can *conduct* electricity, because electrons can move between the layers.

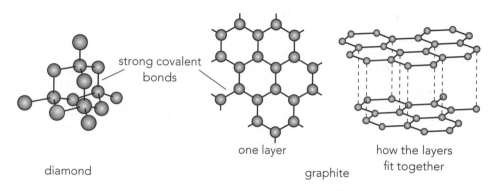

Figure 3.5: The structures of diamond and graphite.

a   ....: to allow electricity to pass through

b   ....: allows light to pass through so we can see through the object

c   ....: light bounces off the surface brightly

d   ...appearance...: how something looks

e   ....: slides easily

f   ....: arranged in the form of a pyramid; each atom is bonded to four others

g   ....: spreading in all three directions

h   ....: arranged in rings of six atoms

i   ....: spreading in just two directions

j   ....: consisting of flat sheets on top of each other

---

LANGUAGE FOCUS

When you talk about the ways in which two things are similar, use *both*.
When you talk about the ways in which two things are different, use *but*.

Both can be placed in front of two nouns to compare them:

<u>Both</u> *diamond and graphite are discussed in this chapter.*

This chapter discusses <u>both</u> *diamond and graphite.*

Both can also go before a verb or after *is/are/was/were*:

Water and carbon dioxide <u>both</u> *contain covalent bonds.*

Water and carbon dioxide are <u>both</u> *covalently bonded.*

To express difference, use *but*. For example, use *but* to contrast using verbs:

Diamond <u>cuts</u> *glass,* <u>but</u> *graphite* <u>does not</u>.

Graphite <u>does not</u> *cut glass,* <u>but</u> *diamond* <u>does</u>.

Molten salts <u>conduct</u> *electricity,* <u>but</u> *solid salts* <u>do not</u>.

Solid salts <u>cannot</u> *conduct electricity,* <u>but</u> *molten salts* <u>can</u>.

Notice that, in this context, where you do not give new information in the second part of the sentence, but only state that A does something and B does not do it, the main verb you use in the first part of the sentence is not repeated after *but*. You only need the opposite form of the auxiliary verb (the short verb used in negatives and questions).

---

9 Complete the following sentences to compare and contrast the properties of diamond and graphite. Follow the structure of the sentences in the Language Focus box.

    a .... diamond and graphite are made of carbon atoms joined by .... to form .... structures.

    b Graphite is dark grey and shiny .... diamond is ....

    c Diamond is very hard .... graphite ....

    d Diamond does not conduct electricity .... graphite ....

    e Write at least one of your own complete sentences contrasting the structures of diamond and graphite. Use *but*.

    ....

    ....

10 Put the following statements in a logical sequence by writing the letters **A–G** in order in the grid. You may wish to write your answers on a piece of paper first.

A Graphite is one form of the element carbon. It is made up of carbon atoms only. These atoms are covalently bonded together in layers. Within the layers each carbon atom is bonded to three other carbons. The atoms are arranged in hexagonal rings of six.

B However, each carbon atom has four outer electrons. This means that there are spare electrons in the structure not used in covalent bonding.

C The layers are lying on top of each other like sheets of paper in a stack and the bonding within the layers is strong. However, the forces between layers are only weak.

D A further property that results from there being no covalent bonds between the layers is the fact that graphite conducts electricity. In the layers each carbon is only sharing three of its outer electrons to make three bonds.

E As the forces between layers are only weak, it is possible for the layers to slide over each other. This is what is happening when a pencil is used.

F Because they are free to move between the layers, the spare, delocalised electrons are able to carry an electric current through a piece of graphite. Graphite is the only non-metal that conducts electricity.

G These spare electrons are able to move between the layers; we say they become 'delocalised'.

Order of statements						
1	2	3	4	5	6	7 ....

After reordering the statements to form a paragraph, write the full paragraph in your notebook.

> **LANGUAGE TIP**
>
> *However* is a formal way of saying 'but' and is often used in scientific writing. Use it to start a sentence, and put a comma after it:
>
> *Diamond and graphite are both forms of carbon. However, some of their properties are very different.*

> Chapter 4

Chemical formulae and equations

IN THIS CHAPTER YOU WILL:

Science skills:

- look at the naming of inorganic chemical compounds and the writing of chemical formulae and equations

- investigate different types of chemical reaction.

English skills:

- develop an understanding of the system for naming inorganic chemical compounds and the criteria for writing word equations

- form plurals for some important chemical terms.

Exercise 4.1 Chemical names and formulae

IN THIS EXERCISE YOU WILL:

Science skills:

- understand the naming of compounds and the writing of chemical formulae.

English skills:

- outline the rules for the systematic naming of compounds, and the exceptions.

KEY WORDS

compound ion: an ion made up of several different atoms covalently bonded together and with an overall charge

LANGUAGE FOCUS

There are two main systems for naming inorganic chemical compounds which are not part of organic chemistry. (See Chapter 18 for the naming of organic compounds.)

1   Compounds containing two elements (simple binary compounds):

Metals and hydrogen are named first, then the ending of the non-metal's name becomes -ide:

sodium chloride   *magnesium oxide*   *iron sulfide*

If the compound contains two non-metals, oxygen or the halogen are named second:

carbon monoxide   *sulfur dioxide*   *phosphorus trichloride*

2   Compounds containing two elements (or more) plus oxygen:

This includes compounds containing compound ions or groups such as carbonate, nitrate, etc. The metal is named first. The non-metal is then named and -ate is added to indicate the presence of oxygen:

aluminium sulfate   *sodium nitrate*   *sodium hydrogen phosphate*

Exceptions:

• compounds with historical names, e.g. *water, ammonia*

• compounds formed from the reaction of ammonia with acids (the ammonium group is named first, e.g. *ammonium* bromide)

• metal hydroxides, e.g. *sodium hydroxide* (these contain two or more elements plus oxygen, but their names end in -ide).

1   Complete the table with the missing information for the simple binary compounds.

Elements present	Name of compound	Formula
potassium and bromine	potassium bromide	KBr_2
zinc and sulfur	....	ZnS
barium and chlorine	....	$BaCl_2$
....	magnesium nitride	Mg_3N_2
....	sulfur trioxide	SO_3
....	nitrogen dioxide	NO_2

2 Complete the table with the missing information for the compounds containing **compound ions**.

Elements present	Name of compound	Formula
sodium, hydrogen, carbon and oxygen	sodium hydrogencarbonate	$NaHCO_3$
zinc, sulfur and oxygen	....	$ZnSO_4$
magnesium, carbon and oxygen	....	$MgCO_3$
....	copper carbonate	$CuCO_3$
....	sodium dihydrogen phosphate	NaH_2PO_4

3 Complete the table, which includes compounds with non-systematic names, with the missing information.

Elements present	Name of compound	Formula
nitrogen and hydrogen	....	NH_3
potassium, hydrogen and oxygen	....	KOH
....	magnesium oxide	MgO
hydrogen and oxygen	....	H_2O
....	ammonium chloride	NH_4Cl
nitrogen, hydrogen and oxygen	....	NH_4NO_3
copper, sulfur and oxygen	....	$CuSO_4$

LANGUAGE TIP

Chemistry terms often come from Latin or Greek. This is true of many chemical symbols; for example, Na (sodium) and Pb (lead) are from Latin *natrium* and *plumbum*; Hg (mercury) is from Greek *hydrargyros*, meaning 'water-silver'.

Exercise 4.2 Atomic structure, bond formation and chemical formulae

IN THIS EXERCISE YOU WILL:

Science skills:

- revise the basic ideas of atomic structure and how these relate to chemical bonding.

English skills:

- become familiar with certain plural forms of key words.

LANGUAGE FOCUS

Most nouns in English form the plural by adding -s or -es to the singular, e.g. *symbol – symbols, gas – gases*. If the noun ends in a consonant + *y*, the plural form changes the -y to -ies, e.g. *valency – valencies*.

However, like chemical symbols, some technical words take their plural form from Latin or Greek. This means that some scientific plurals are formed differently. Look at these patterns:

Singular noun with -us → plural with -i: e.g. *nucleus – nuclei*

Singular noun with -a → plural with -ae: e.g. *formula – formulae*

Singular noun with -um → plural with -a: e.g. *spectrum – spectra; datum – data*

Singular noun with -is → plural with -es: e.g. *analysis – analyses; axis – axes*

Also, singular nouns *criterion* and *phenomenon* → *criteria* and *phenomena*

Remember to use the correct form of the verb with plurals.

4   a   Complete the following paragraph using these words.

   electrons   nuclei   nucleus   proton   protons

The way that the chemical elements combine depends on the structure of the atoms involved. Every atom is made up of a central .... surrounded by orbiting .... Remember that all the atoms of a particular element have the same number of .... in their .... The number of protons in the .... of an atom is known as the .... number (or atomic number) of the element. The atomic number of an element defines the position of the element in the Periodic Table.

   b   Complete the following paragraphs using the words given.

   combining   electrons   formula   formulae

   power   valencies

The electrons of an atom orbit around the nucleus in different shells (energy levels). The most important .... are those in the outer shell. These are the electrons used to make chemical bonds between atoms. The outer electrons are sometimes known as the valency electrons. The combining .... (valency) of an atom is the number of chemical bonds an atom can make. The .... powers of the elements depend on the number of .... in the outer shell (see Table 4.1).

LANGUAGE TIP

Atoms of each element have a combining power, sometimes known as their valency. Valencies can be used to work out the formulae of compounds. The term valency is not required knowledge.

Group in Periodic Table	I	II	III	IV	V	VI	VII	VIII
Number of outer electrons	1	2	3	4	5	6	7	8
Combining power (valency)	1	2	3	4	3	2	1	0

Table 4.1: The relationship between group number and the outer electrons in an atom.

Every chemical substance has a chemical formula. The chemical .... of a compound tells us which elements are present, and also how many of each type of atom are combined. The chemical .... of compounds can be worked out if we know the .... of the elements present. Chemical formulae are important when we need to write equations for the reactions that take place between substances.

Exercise 4.3 Chemical reactions and equations

IN THIS EXERCISE YOU WILL:

Science skills:

- distinguish a chemical reaction from a physical change and investigate different types of chemical reactions.

English skills:

- interpret descriptions of chemical reactions and write word equations for them.

KEY WORDS

word equation: a summary of a chemical reaction using the chemical names of the reactants and products

5   Read the following text about Mahmoud's experiment, then use the words in *italics* to complete the table. One example has been done for you.

> Mahmoud is in the laboratory. From the cupboard of *reagents*, he selects a strip of magnesium. He holds the magnesium in a Bunsen burner flame with a pair of tongs. The magnesium burns with a bright white flame. Afterwards, a white powder remains.
>
> Mahmoud knows a *chemical reaction* has taken place because a new substance has formed. This is different from a *physical change*. The *reactants* were magnesium and oxygen and the *product* is magnesium oxide.

Definition	Term
a change in which new substances are produced	....
the substances that react together in a chemical reaction	....
the chemicals available in a laboratory	....
the substance formed in a chemical reaction	..........product..........
a change in which the substances remain the same – no new substances are formed	....

6   Look at the following descriptions. For each, decide whether it is a *physical change* or a *chemical reaction*. Write the correct term on the line below each description.

a   Water in a kettle boils to produce steam and water vapour.

....

b   The steel body of a car rusts and holes appear.

....

c   Ammonium dichromate decomposes, producing a lot of heat and nitrogen gas.

....

d   An egg is cooked in an iron frying pan.

....

e   A banana freezes solid when placed in liquid nitrogen.

....

LANGUAGE FOCUS

A chemical equation is a summary of what has taken place in a reaction. The simplest form of chemical equation is a **word equation**. A word equation uses the names of the reactants and products linked by an arrow. The basic structure of any chemical equation is:

reactants → products

Sometimes, you will need to produce a word equation. You will be given a description of the reaction, which will contain the information you need to construct the word equation.

Look at these two examples of how reactions are re-expressed as word equations.

Description: *Hydrogen gas is mixed with oxygen gas and a spark is used to ignite them. A loud explosion and brief flame are produced. Water vapour is the single product.*

Word equation: *hydrogen + oxygen → water*

In the word equation, you only need the names of substances (reactants and products), not the state they are in. Therefore, write 'hydrogen', not 'hydrogen gas'.

The spark and flame are not in the equation as they are not chemicals.

Description: *Green powdered copper carbonate is heated in a test-tube. The powder becomes black copper oxide, and a gas which turns limewater cloudy is produced.*

Word equation: *copper carbonate $\xrightarrow{\text{heat}}$ copper oxide + carbon dioxide*

Here you must remember the 'gas... produced' in the description is carbon dioxide.

The heat causing the reaction is not included in the equation, but it is written above the arrow to show it is necessary to produce the reaction. It is important, here, to show the use of heat in this way, as it is a thermal decomposition reaction.

7   Read the following descriptions, then write the word equations for the reactions taking place.

a   Small pieces of zinc metal are added to hydrochloric acid solution. A strong reaction takes place and bubbles of hydrogen gas are given off. A colourless solution of zinc chloride is left at the end.

Word equation: ....

b   Glucose is produced in the green leaves of plants. The leaves take in carbon dioxide from the air, which reacts with water in the leaf. Oxygen gas is also produced.

Word equation: ....

8 **a**   The 'model equation' in Figure 4.1 describes the combustion of methane.

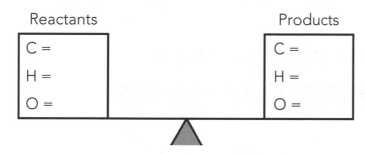

Figure 4.1: The combustion of methane.

i   Write the word equation for this reaction.

....

ii Count the number of each type of atom on the reactants and products side of the equation and enter the numbers into the diagram.

Reactants   Products

C =   C =

H =   H =

O =   O =

What do you notice about the number of atoms of each element on each side of the equation?

....

This is what we mean when we say that an equation is 'balanced'. When we write equations using formulae, we can also include state symbols after each reactant and product. In this case we need the following: (g) = gas and (l) = liquid.

iii Using the information in part **ii**, write the balanced symbol equation for the reaction, including state symbols.

....

LANGUAGE TIP

Stoichiometry describes the relationships between the amounts of reactants and products during chemical reactions. It is made from two Greek words: *stoicheion* (element) and *metron* (measure). Stoichiometric coefficients are the numbers before the formulae in an equation that you alter to balance an equation.

Chemical calculations

Exercise 5.1 Relative atomic masses

KEY WORDS

relative atomic mass (A_r): the average mass of naturally occurring atoms of an element on a scale where an atom of carbon-12 has a mass of exactly 12 units

1   On the scale of **relative atomic masses**, copper has a mass of 64.

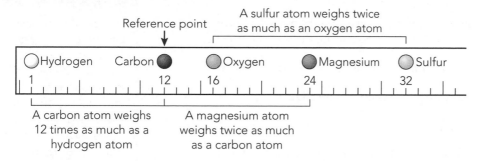

Figure 5.1: Relating the masses of atoms to carbon-12 produces a scale of useful values.

a   Circle the correct word to complete the following sentences comparing copper and the atoms shown in Figure 5.1.

   i   Copper atoms have a mass which is **half / twice** the mass of a sulfur atom.

   ii   A magnesium atom has **double / half** the mass of a carbon atom.

   iii   An oxygen atom has a mass that is four times **less / greater** than a copper atom.

   iv   A carbon atom has **twice / half** the mass of a magnesium atom.

   v   A copper atom has a mass which is **a quarter / four times** that of an oxygen atom.

LANGUAGE FOCUS

When you need to compare the mass, volume, length, etc., of two things, you can use some of the expressions in Figure 5.1.

It (weighs) _twice / X times as much as_ …

This is a useful expression for comparing two measurements*. You can also say:

X weighs _half as much as_ Y.

X weighs _(12) times less than_ Y.

X weighs _double the_ mass of Y.

X weighs _half the_ mass of Y.

X weighs _a third/quarter of_ the mass of Y.

The mass of X _is a third/quarter that of_ Y. ('That' refers to 'mass', in this sentence.)

We can also express the statements in Figure 5.1 in a different way:

The mass of a carbon atom is 12 _times greater than_ the mass of a hydrogen atom.

A sulfur atom weighs two _times more than_ an oxygen atom.

A magnesium atom has a mass two _times greater than_ a carbon atom.

The mass of a carbon atom _is half that of_ a magnesium atom.

These are different ways of saying the same thing as is written in Figure 5.1.

*If you compare units of amount or measurement, e.g. grams, use _many_ instead of _much_.

b Carbon has a relative atomic mass (A_r) of 12. Hydrogen has a relative atomic mass (A_r) of 1.

The following passage uses the idea of measuring the masses of atoms relative to a standard. Complete the passage using the words in the box.

double	**four**	**helium**	**lithium**	**third**	**three**
	twenty-four		**twice**	**relative**	

A magnesium atom is found to be ($2\times$) .... as heavy as a carbon atom. That means that the mass of a magnesium atom is .... that of carbon. If we say that carbon has a mass of twelve, then magnesium has a relative mass of (2×12) ....

A helium atom has a mass which is only a ($\frac{1}{3}$) .... of that of a carbon atom. It has a .... mass of just four.

Exercise 5.2 Molecular mass and percentage composition

IN THIS EXERCISE YOU WILL:

Science skills:

- look at how relative molecular or formula masses are used to calculate the percentage composition of a compound.

English skills:

- become familiar with the language of mathematical processes and equations.

KEY WORDS

relative formula mass (M_r): the sum of all the relative atomic masses of all the atoms present in a 'formula unit' of a substance

LANGUAGE FOCUS

When you write a mathematical operation, you use the international symbols +, −, ×, ÷, =, etc. However, when you speak, you need to know how to express those operations in words. There are two ways to do this:

1   To explain a mathematical operation, use *add* (+), *subtract* (−), *multiply by* (×) and *divide by* (÷). There are different expressions for =:

Add both numbers together, then divide by two. <u>This gives you</u> the average.

<u>Calculate</u> the average by adding both numbers together, then dividing the result by two.

Multiply thirty-two by five. <u>This will give you</u> the mass of five moles of sulfur.

If you subtract six from fourteen and then multiply the result by three <u>you get</u> twenty-four.

<u>To work out</u> the mass number of an atom, you need to add together the number of protons and neutrons present.

2   When you read an equation, say *plus* (+), *minus* (−), *times* (×), *over/into* (÷) and *equals* or *is* (=). Use the pronunciation button on a good online dictionary to help you say these words correctly.

Sixteen times two <u>plus</u> eight <u>equals</u> forty.

Forty <u>minus</u> twenty-five percent <u>is</u> thirty.

Forty over four <u>equals</u> ten, times three <u>equals</u> thirty.

Four <u>into</u> forty <u>equals</u> ten, times three <u>is</u> thirty.

LANGUAGE TIP

Apart from the terms for essential mathematical operations, other useful mathematical terms include *average*, *calculate*, *the result*, *work out*, *percent* and *percentage*. Try to write your own memorable example sentences using these words to help you remember them.

2   Ammonium nitrate has the formula NH_4NO_3 (see Table 5.1). It is a very important fertiliser for adding nitrogen to the soil to help plants grow. Knowing the atomic masses of each atom, we can work out the percentage (%) of nitrogen in a compound such as ammonium nitrate.

NH_4NO_3	2 N atoms	4 H atoms	3 O atoms	Total mass = 28 + 4 + 48 = **80**
	$2 \times 14 = 28$	$4 \times 1 = 4$	$3 \times 16 = 48$	

Table 5.1: Calculating the relative formula mass of ammonium nitrate.

To calculate the percentage of nitrogen in ammonium nitrate, we perform the following steps:

* multiply the total mass of nitrogen in the formula by 100
* divide the result by the **relative formula mass** of ammonium nitrate (see Table 5.1).

a Write the formula needed to calculate the percentage of nitrogen in ammonium nitrate.

....

b Use the values in Table 5.1 to calculate the percentage of nitrogen in ammonium nitrate.

....

This means that every 100 g of ammonium nitrate contains

.... g nitrogen.

Exercise 5.3 Isotopes and atomic masses

IN THIS EXERCISE YOU WILL:

Science skills:

- understand that the value for the relative atomic mass must take into account the different isotopes of an element.

English skills:

- express the important terms that define atomic masses and their relationship to atomic structure.

KEY WORDS

relative molecular mass (M_r): the sum of all the relative atomic masses of the atoms present in a molecule

3 In the following grid, draw lines to match the terms about atomic and formula masses with their definitions. One example has been done for you. Then complete the definitions using words from the box.

average   mass   molecule   neutrons

nucleon   protons

Chemical term	Definition
mass number	a carbon-12 atom is given a .... of exactly 12
the standard for measuring relative atomic mass	the number of .... and .... in the nucleus of an atom; also called the nucleon number
relative atomic mass, A_r	the sum of all the relative atomic masses for the atoms in a .... ; use only for covalent substances
isotopes	atoms of the same element with different .... numbers; they have different numbers of neutrons
relative molecular (or formula) mass, M_r	the .... mass of an atom of an element, using a scale where an atom of carbon-12 has a mass of exactly 12

4 The following sentences describe the ratio of the different types of chlorine atoms present in a natural sample of the gas. Complete the sentences with the words *atoms* (×2) and *isotopes* (×3) so that they make correct sense.

a A natural sample of chlorine gas contains two ...., chlorine-35 and chlorine-37. The proportions of these two .... are 75% and 25%.

b If a sample of chlorine contains 1000 atoms, there will be 750 .... of chlorine-35 and 250 .... of chlorine-37. The two .... are present in the ratio 3:1.

Exercise 5.4 Counting particles – the mole

IN THIS EXERCISE YOU WILL:

Science skills:

- develop an understanding of the concept of the mole as a measure of amount of substance.

English skills:

- use the key terms you have met so far in this chapter.

5 Match the following sentence halves to make key definitions of the mole and Avogadro's constant. Write the full definitions in the space provided.

	Start of sentence	End of sentence
a	One mole of a substance has…	…6.02×10^{23} atoms, molecules or other characteristic particles.
b	Avogadro's constant is the…	…a mass equal to the molecular (or formula) mass of the substance in grams.
c	One mole of a substance contains…	…number of atoms, molecules or characteristic particles in one mole of a substance.
d	Avogadro's constant =…	…6.02×10^{23} (Avogadro's constant) atoms, molecules or characteristic particles.

a ....

....

b ....

....

c ....

....

d ....

....

6 Complete the missing information in the following text.

The concept of the mole is useful. It means that chemical equations tell us not only what the products of a reaction are; they also tell us how much product we should expect to get.

Magnesium metal burns in oxygen with a bright white light. The chemical equation (balanced symbol equation) for the reaction gives a lot of information.

$$2Mg \quad + \quad O_2 \quad \rightarrow \quad 2MgO$$

$\quad\quad$ 2 $\quad\quad\quad$ 1

$\quad$ atoms $\quad$ molecule

This equation tells you that two atoms of magnesium react with .... molecule(s) of oxygen.

If we work in moles, we can scale this up to levels of material we can actually use. The equation is telling us that: .... moles of magnesium react with 1 mole of oxygen molecules to give .... moles of magnesium oxide.

> **LANGUAGE TIP**
>
> Questions in chemistry often start with *How much* or *How many*. They mean the same thing and ask for quantity. However, *many* is used for things you can count (molecules, atoms, substances) and *much* is used for things you cannot count (energy, mass, time).

We know how much 1 mole of each substance weighs (A_r: Mg = 24, O = 16), so we can write:

$$2Mg \quad + \quad O_2 \quad \rightarrow \quad 2MgO$$

$$2 \times 24 = \text{........} g \quad + \quad 32\,g \quad \rightarrow \quad \text{........} g$$

Using information from the equation for the reaction, 0.48 g of magnesium will produce .... g of magnesium oxide when burnt completely in oxygen.

7   The mathematical equation that relates the mass of a substance (in grams) to the number of moles present is:

$$\text{number of moles} = \frac{\text{mass}}{\text{molar mass}}$$

If two of these values are known, the third can be calculated by rearranging this equation.

Work in pairs; one partner is **A**, one is **B**. Cover your partner's half of the table, which shows different rearrangements of the equation above. Take turns to read the equation in your *Say* box. Listen to your partner and write what you hear, as an equation, in your *Listen and write* box.

A	B
Say: molar mass = mass / number of moles	Listen and write: ....
Listen and write:	Say: mass = molar mass × number of moles

Exercise 5.5 Making solutions

IN THIS EXERCISE YOU WILL:

Science skills:

*   investigate the nature of solutions in terms of their constituent parts and how solutions can be prepared.

English skills:

*   consider the formation of different words from the same root, and use key vocabulary to write a set of instructions.

KEY WORD

solubility: a measure of how much of a solute dissolves in a solvent at a particular temperature

---

LANGUAGE FOCUS

Forming the correct word from 'root' words is always important, but it is essential in scientific English. The end of a word or suffix often indicates if it is a noun (n), an adjective (adj) or a verb (v), for example.

it dissolves (v present simple), *soluble* (adj), *solution* (n), *cylinder* (n), *cylindrical* (adj)

You can often guess the general meaning of words from the root – the part before the suffix – which can help you understand new words.

aquarium (n), *aquatic* (adj), *aqueous* (adj) – you can guess from *aquarium* the connection with *water*.

Sometimes in science, the suffix can also tell you about meaning:

solvent: liquid that dissolves solids, a *dissolving* liquid

solute: the solid dissolved in the liquid, a *dissolved* solid

---

8 a Circle the correct options in the following passages about constituent parts of solutions.

In general terms, the solid that dissolves in the liquid is called the **solvent / solute**. The liquid in which the solid dissolves is called the **solvent / solute**.

If a substance dissolves in a solvent, it is said to be **insoluble / soluble**: if it does not dissolve, it is **insoluble / soluble**. A **dilute / concentrated** solution contains a small proportion of solute. A **dilute / concentrated** solution contains a high proportion of solute.

b Read the following steps for making a saturated solution of sodium chloride at room temperature.

Put a tick beside the sentences that are instructions and underline the command words in those sentences.

Use a balance to measure out 1.0 g of sodium chloride and then add the solid to the water in the beaker. ☐

Measure 50 cm³ of distilled water in a measuring cylinder and pour it into a beaker. ☐

Carry on adding small portions of salt to the solution until no more dissolves. ☐

This is a saturated solution. ☐

LANGUAGE TIP

Remember you can say or write instructions easily by using any action verb to start a sentence: *Copy the Periodic Table. Measure the solvent. Light the Bunsen burner.*

To get more solid to dissolve, the temperature must be increased. ☐

Stir the mixture with a glass rod until all the salt has dissolved. ☐

The concentration of sodium chloride in a saturated solution is a measure of its **solubility** at that temperature. ☐

c   Harsha and Jenna needed to prepare $100\,cm^3$ of a solution of copper(II) sulfate in water. This is the report they wrote.

> We took a $100\,cm^3$ measuring cylinder and filled it approximately half full with distilled water. We used a balance to carefully measure out $1.0\,g$ of copper sulfate. Using a small filter funnel, we poured the solid into the measuring cylinder. We washed out any remaining solid on the filter funnel with a little distilled water. We shook the cylinder gently until all the solid had dissolved. We then added more distilled water to the solution, shaking it gently to make sure the solution was well mixed, until the level of the solution was exactly at the $100\,cm^3$ mark on the neck of the cylinder.

From their report, write a series of practical instructions that other students could follow. Write your instructions in the space provided. The first and last steps have been started for you.

1   Take a $100\,cm^3$ measuring cylinder. Fill ....

....

2   ....

....

3   ....

....

4   ....

....

5   ....

....

6   With gentle shaking, add ....

....

> Chapter 6
Electrochemistry

IN THIS CHAPTER YOU WILL:

Science skills:

- describe the electrolysis of ionic compounds and the generation of electricity using a hydrogen–oxygen fuel cell

- investigate electrical conductivity in metals.

English skills:

- look at the use of verbs to describe chemical processes

- learn how to use linkers to connect two ideas in a sentence to show cause or consequence.

Exercise 6.1 Electrolysis of lead bromide

IN THIS EXERCISE YOU WILL:

Science skills:

- describe the basic ideas involved in electrolysis.

English skills:

- practise the use of the present simple active and passive.

KEY WORDS

anode: the electrode in any type of cell at which oxidation (the loss of electrons) takes place – in electrolysis it is the positive electrode

cathode: the electrode in any type of cell at which reduction (the gain of electrons) takes place; in electrolysis it is the negative electrode

electrolysis: the breakdown of an ionic compound, molten or in aqueous solution, by the use of electricity

electrolyte: an ionic compound that will conduct electricity when it is molten or dissolved in water; electrolytes will not conduct electricity when solid

1 a The verbs listed are important when we describe what is taking place during **electrolysis**. Write each verb with its definition.

   to decompose   to discharge   to electrolyse   to split

   i .... : to separate something into parts

   ii .... : to cause a compound to react by passing an electric current through it

   iii .... : to cause an ion to lose its charge

   iv .... : to break down a substance into simpler substances

   b Which two words in part **a** have similar meanings?

   ....

LANGUAGE TIP

Some English verbs can add *up* to mean 'completely', e.g. *split up* means to fully separate, to split into parts; *break up* can be similar. *Clean up* means to clean everything, e.g. after an experiment.

LANGUAGE FOCUS

When you write about chemical processes in general, use the present simple (see Chapter 3). When the scientist or 'thing' carrying out the action is not important to know or is unknown, use the passive form of the verb, instead of the active form, because this makes the process the most important thing in the sentence.

The passive is very frequent in scientific writing and is easy to form:

   They usually make <u>bimetallic strips</u> with steel and copper. = present active

   <u>Bimetallic strips</u> are usually made with steel and copper. = present passive.

You do not know who *They* are, so use the passive, like this:

1 The object of the active sentence becomes the subject at the start of the passive sentence.

2 Add *is, are, (am), is not* or *are not* (or *am not*).

3 Then add the past participle of the verb.

The past participle of regular verbs ends with *-ed* and looks the same as the past tense.

The past participle of irregular verbs is the third 'column' when you look at a verb table:

bring	brought	*brought*
give	gave	*given*
make	made	*made*
put	put	*put*

c   Complete the following paragraphs using the correct form of the verbs given. Choose from the present simple active or passive. The first one has been done for you.

In electrolysis, an ionic compound (an **electrolyte**) (*decompose*) _is decomposed_ by an electric current passing through it. The electrolyte must be either a liquid (molten) or dissolved in water. This is important as the ions must be able to move to the electrodes. Electrolysis (*carry out*) .... in an electrolytic cell and the electrodes (*connect*) .... to a source of direct current. One electrode (*become*) .... positively charged (the **anode**), the other negatively charged (the **cathode**). When ions (*reach*) .... the electrodes, they (*discharge*) .... A simple electrolyte like lead bromide (*split*) .... into its elements during electrolysis.

Positive ions (*move*) .... towards the cathode when the current (*switch on*) .... Because of this, positive ions are sometimes called cations. Negative ions are called anions because they (*move*) .... to the anode when the current is switched on.

When the positive ions reach the cathode, they gain electrons. We say that reduction (*occur*) .... at the cathode. At the other electrode the negative ions (*lose*) .... electrons. The negative ions (*oxidise*) .... at the anode.

d   Complete the descriptions of the changes taking place during the electrolysis of molten lead bromide, using the correct active or passive form of the verbs. Then complete the balanced electrode equation at the end of each description. Use Figure 6.1 and the information in part **c** to help you.

discharge (×2)   form (×2)   gain (×2)   lose (×2)   move (×2)

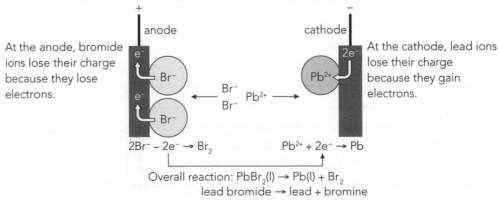

Electrons move around the circuit from one electrode to the other.

At the anode, bromide ions lose their charge because they lose electrons.

At the cathode, lead ions lose their charge because they gain electrons.

$2Br^- - 2e^- \rightarrow Br_2$

$Pb^{2+} + 2e^- \rightarrow Pb$

Overall reaction: $PbBr_2(l) \rightarrow Pb(l) + Br_2$
lead bromide → lead + bromine

Figure 6.1: The electrolysis of molten lead bromide.

> **LANGUAGE TIP**
>
> *Liquid* and *aqueous* are often confused but they are, in fact, quite different. *Liquid* is a state and can describe anything in that state, e.g. *liquid chocolate, liquid gold.* *Aqueous* is related to *aqua* (*water* in Latin) and means *made with or containing water.* In chemistry, the state symbol (aq) means *in solution in water.*

i   The movement of the lead ions (Pb^{2+}) and their reaction at the electrode.

The lead ions are positively charged so they .... to

the cathode. Here these ions .... because they

.... electrons. This is a reduction reaction because electrons

.... Liquid lead .... at this electrode.

$$Pb^{2+} + \text{........................} \rightarrow Pb$$

ii   The movement of the bromide ions (Br^-) and their reaction at the electrode.

Bromide ions are negatively charged and so they ....

towards the anode. Here these ions .... because they

.... electrons. This is an oxidation reaction because

electrons .... Bromine gas .... at

this electrode.

$$2Br^- - 2e^- \rightarrow \text{........................}$$

Exercise 6.2 Testing electrical conductivity

IN THIS EXERCISE YOU WILL:

Science skills:

• define the different types of electrical conductivity that can occur.

English skills:

• apply the different technical terms used in discussing electrical conductivity.

KEY WORDS

ceramic: material such as pottery made from inorganic chemicals by high-temperature processing

electrical conductor: a substance that conducts electricity but is not chemically changed in the process

insulator: a substance that does not conduct electricity

2 a The diagram shows the circuit diagram of the apparatus used to test whether a solid conducts electricity. Complete the labels in the diagram and draw an arrow to show the direction of flow of electrons.

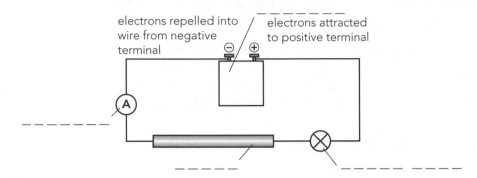

electrons repelled into wire from negative terminal

electrons attracted to positive terminal

b i Different solids **A–E** were tested in the apparatus shown in the diagram. Complete the table to show if the substance is an **electrical conductor** or **insulator**. Then answer the questions that follow.

Solid	Appearance of solid	Test result	Conductor or insulator
A	shiny, light grey rod	bulb lit up and current recorded	conductor
B	hard brown rod	bulb did not light up and no current recorded	....
C	black rod	bulb lit up and current recorded	....
D	yellow block	bulb did not light up and no current recorded	....
E	red–brown strip	bulb lit up and current recorded	....

ii Which of these solids could be a graphite rod?.............................

iii Which of these solids are metals?.............................

iv Which of these solids could be made of **ceramic** material?.....................

v Which solid could be sulfur?.............................

Exercise 6.3 Types of electrical conductivity

IN THIS EXERCISE YOU WILL:

Science skill:

• discuss how the different types of electrical conductivity take place.

English skills:

• learn how to construct sentences that link ideas to their cause or consequences.

LANGUAGE FOCUS

When you write well, you use special words, known as connectives or linkers, to connect two ideas in a sentence; these words show a relationship between the two parts. In chemistry, you often need to show the connection between cause and consequence.

The simplest word to introduce cause is *because*. The simplest word to introduce consequence is *so* (see Chapter 1). However, there are more scientific words you can use, including *as* and *therefore*:

As the movement of ions is a true phenomenon, electrolysis happens.
(*As* + cause, consequence)

Electrolysis happens in solutions, as cations and anions move in opposite directions. (consequence, *as* + cause)

Atomic theory about electrons is true. Therefore, the formation of chemical bonds happens. (cause, *Therefore*, + consequence)

Although you can use *as* at the start of a sentence or in the middle, *therefore* generally goes before the second piece of information.

When you use *as*, you need a comma (,) at the end of the phrase.

When you use *Therefore*, you need a comma after it.

3   a   Complete the following statements about electrical conductivity and electrolysis by drawing lines to link phrases **1–4** with phrases **A–D**.

1	None of the electrons in the structure of non-metals are free to move, …		**A**	… solid lead(II) bromide does not conduct electricity.
2	As the ions present in a solid salt are held in fixed positions in the structure and are not free to move, …		**B**	… Therefore, metallic elements and alloys conduct electricity.
3	As the ions present in a molten liquid electrolyte are free to move, …		**C**	… the non-metal, sulfur, does not conduct electricity.
4	There are free mobile electrons in the structure of a metal. …		**D**	… the molten salt, lead(II) bromide, conducts electricity.

   b   Complete the following sentences which link causes and consequences. Use *as* or *therefore*.

   i   .... copper and gold are metals, they both conduct electricity well.

   ii   A block of sulfur does not conduct electricity. ...., it cannot be a metal.

iii .... sodium chloride contains two elements chemically combined, it must be a compound and not just a mixture.

iv Copper is a very good conductor of electricity. ...., it can be widely used in electrical wiring in the home.

v .... passing an electric current through molten zinc chloride produces chlorine gas, we can conclude that electrolysis has taken place.

Exercise 6.4 Hydrogen–oxygen fuel cells

IN THIS EXERCISE YOU WILL:

Science skills:

• consider the differences between an electrolytic cell and a fuel cell.

English skills:

• develop further familiarity with the key vocabulary used when discussing electrical conductivity.

4 a Hydrogen–oxygen fuel cells are a possible alternative to engines that use diesel as fuel.

Complete the following statements using the words given (two words are not needed).

compound   elements   hydrogen   metals

opposite   oxygen   produces   water

i In an electrolytic cell, an electric current is used to produce a chemical reaction that splits a compound into its .... An electrolytic cell uses electrical energy.

ii A hydrogen fuel cell uses a chemical reaction that combines two elements together to produce a .... A fuel cell .... electrical energy.

iii In a hydrogen–oxygen fuel cell, hydrogen reacts with .... to produce ....

Now complete the balanced equation for the reaction:

.... H_2 + ... → .... H_2O

iv A fuel cell is the .... of an electrolytic cell.

b The topic of electrolysis involves some new, important words and ideas. Complete the crossword using the clues given.

Across

1 This is formed by a molten binary compound at the electrodes during electrolysis

3 The charge on the cathode in electrolysis

6 The non-polluting product from a hydrogen–oxygen fuel cell

9 The number of electrons gained by lead ions in electrolysis

10 The name for the overall reaction taking place at the electrodes during electrolysis

12 An inert substance used for electrodes

15 The name for the process of coating an object with a metal by electrolysis

18 The gas formed at the positive electrode in electrolysis of dilute sulfuric acid

Down

2 The apparatus in which electrolysis takes place

4 The source of voltage for powering electrolysis

5 Compounds do this during electrolysis

7 The liquid that conducts electricity in electrolysis

8 The particles that move through the liquid in electrolysis

11 The fuel used in fuel cells to drive cars

13 The type of reaction taking place at the positive electrode in electrolysis

14 The metal purified by electrolysis for electrical wiring

16 The element formed at the cathode in the electrolysis of lead bromide

17 The positive electrode in electrolysis

Chemical energetics

Science skills:

- describe the energy changes involved in the progress of chemical reactions

- look at the difference between exothermic and endothermic processes and chemical reactions.

English skills:

- use prepositions when expressing differences between substances or situations

- use linkers to show relationships between ideas.

Exercise 7.1 Physical and chemical changes

IN THIS EXERCISE YOU WILL:

Science skills:

- understand the difference between a chemical reaction and a physical change.

English skills:

- express a difference between situations and between the properties of substances.

KEY WORDS

chemical reaction (change): a change in which a new substance is formed

physical change: a change in the physical state of a substance or the physical nature of a situation that does not involve a change in the chemical substance(s) present

1   Ice, snow and water look different, but they are all made of water molecules (H_2O). They are different physical forms of the same substance, existing under different conditions of temperature and pressure. One form can change into another if the conditions change. In such physical changes, no new chemical substances are formed.

LANGUAGE FOCUS

When you want to talk about differences, for example between physical forms, you need to know which prepositions to use with the words *difference* and *different*. 'Difference' works with *between*, but 'different' works with *from* or *to*. In this context, *from* and *to* mean the same thing:

One <u>difference</u> <u>between</u> diamond and graphite is that diamond is hard but graphite is soft.

There are considerable <u>differences</u> <u>between</u> diamond and graphite.

The chemical nature of olive oil soap is <u>different</u> <u>from/to</u> olive oil.

Olive oil soap has a <u>different</u> chemical nature <u>from/to</u> olive oil.

Ice looks and feels <u>different</u> <u>from/to</u> its liquid state.

Where you want to express no difference, use *same* with *as*:

Water has the <u>same</u> chemical formula <u>as</u> ice.

a   Complete the following sentences, using words from the Language Focus box.

   i   Ice is water in a .... physical state .... the
       liquid that we drink.

   ii   The difference .... ice and water is that ice is a solid.

   iii   Ice exists under .... conditions ....
        liquid water.

   iv   Water and water vapour have the .... chemical formula
        .... ice, so melting and evaporation must be
        physical changes.

b   Separate the words in the sentences below to find sentences that describe the
    main differences between **chemical reactions (changes)**. Then write the sentences on the
    lines provided.

    Chemical changes:

    Themajorfeatureofachemicalchange,orreaction,isthatnewsubstancesaremadeduringthereaction.
    Manyreactionsbut,notall,aredifficultoreverse.
    Duringachemicalreaction,energycanbegivenoutortakenin.Mostreactionsgiveoutenergy.

    *   ....
        ....

    *   ....
        ....

    *   ....
        ....

Exercise 7.2 Exothermic and endothermic chemical reactions

IN THIS EXERCISE YOU WILL:

Science skills:

- describe how heat energy is transferred between the chemical system and the surroundings during a chemical reaction.

English skills:

- use linkers to express the consequences of a change in conditions or circumstances.

KEY WORDS

endothermic change: a process or chemical reaction which takes in heat from the surroundings.
ΔH for an endothermic change has a positive value.

exothermic change: a process or chemical reaction in which heat energy is produced and released to the surroundings.
ΔH for an exothermic change has a negative value.

LANGUAGE FOCUS

As you saw in Chapters 1 and 6, there are various linkers (connectives) that you can use to link cause and consequence. You can also use the same linkers to connect reason and deduction. When you use them in this way, the deduction often includes the verb *must*:

Because / As water consists of hydrogen and oxygen, oxygen <u>must be</u> the most abundant element in the human body by mass.

Water consists of hydrogen and oxygen, <u>so</u> oxygen <u>must be</u> the most abundant element in the human body by mass.

Water consists of hydrogen and oxygen. <u>Therefore</u>, oxygen <u>must be</u> the most abundant element in the human body by mass.

Other linkers that you can use in place of *because* and that are appropriate for scientific writing are *given that* and *since*. They are used at the start or in the middle of the sentence:

<u>Given that / Since</u> water consists of hydrogen and oxygen, oxygen must be the most abundant element in the human body by mass.

Another linker you can use in place of *Therefore*, is *For this reason,*:

Water consists of hydrogen and oxygen. <u>For this reason</u>, oxygen must be the most abundant element in the human body by mass.

2 To decide whether a particular change is physical or chemical, you need to think about the change and its results. Circle the correct linker in the sentences **a–e**, then complete the sentences using *physical change* or *chemical reaction*.

a **For this reason, / Given that** mixing sulfuric acid and sodium hydroxide solutions produces new chemical substances, it must be a ....

b **Since / Therefore,** the ice produced from freezing a sample of water can be easily thawed back to liquid water, this process must be a ....

c Rusting involves the production of red-brown iron(III) oxide and the process cannot be reversed. **For this reason, / Since** this must be a ....

d **For this reason, / Given that** the salt dissolved in water in a salt solution can be obtained from the solution by evaporation, making the solution must be a ....

e Burning methane gas during cooking produces a lot of heat and gives off carbon dioxide and water vapour. **For this reason, / Since** this must be a

....

3 During a chemical reaction, there is always an energy change. Most reactions release (*give out*) heat energy; they are **exothermic**. However, there are a few reactions that absorb (*take in*) heat from the surroundings; they are **endothermic**. Use the information in Figure 7.1 to identify which reaction is exothermic, and which is endothermic.

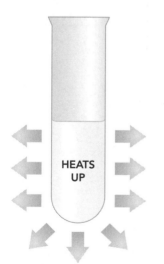 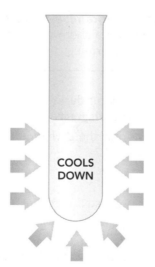

a This reaction gives out heat. This warms the mixture and then heat is released to the surroundings.

b This reaction takes in heat. This cools the mixture and then heat is absorbed from the surroundings.

Figure 7.1: Two different reactions.

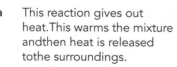

a .... thermic   b .... thermic

Exercise 7.3 Reaction pathways and bond energies

IN THIS EXERCISE YOU WILL:

Science skills:

- understand that energy is given out when chemical bonds are formed, while energy is needed to break bonds, and that activation energy is the energy required to start a chemical reaction.

English skills:

- practise language terms used for discussing the energy changes involved in a chemical reaction.

KEY WORDS

activation energy (E_a): the minimum energy required to start a chemical reaction – for a reaction to take place the colliding particles must possess at least this amount of energy

enthalpy change (ΔH): the heat change during the course of a reaction (also known as heat of reaction); can be either exothermic (a negative value) or endothermic (a positive value)

reaction pathway diagram (energy level diagram): a diagram that shows the energy levels of the reactants and products in a chemical reaction and shows whether the reaction is exothermic or endothermic

4 Exothermic and endothermic changes that occur during reactions can be shown using **reaction pathway diagrams (energy level diagrams)**.

  a Complete the following bullet points describing what the following diagrams show.

  Such diagrams show:

- heat energy on the .... axis (*y*-axis) with the levels for the

  reactants and .... shown, as in the diagram

- the 'reaction pathway' (........................ of reaction) on the

  .... axis (*x*-axis), with reactants on the left and products on

  the right

- the energy change indicated by an arrow (upward or downward) between

  the reactants and products.

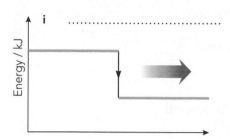

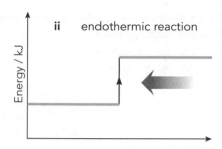

b Label the diagrams using the words listed. Some words may be used more than once.

exothermic reaction   **heat given out**   **heat taken in**

products   **progress of reaction**   **reactants**

5 Chemical reactions always involve chemical bonds that are broken in the reactants before new bonds are formed to make the products. The energies involved in these two processes determine whether reactions are exothermic or endothermic.

a Two ideas are essential to understanding the energy changes involved during a chemical reaction:

- Breaking a bond always requires energy.
- Making a bond always gives out energy.

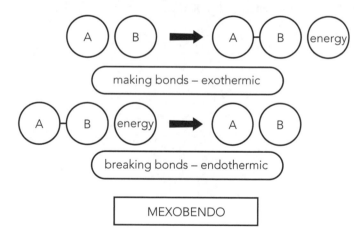

Figure 7.2: A memory aid for the bond changes during a chemical reaction.

State what the following parts of the memory aid 'MEXOBENDO' (Figure 7.2) mean:

i M   ....

ii B   ....

iii EXO   ....

iv ENDO   ....

b   Read the following information. Then, using the energy values given, calculate the **enthalpy change** of reaction.

The heat change of a chemical reaction is known as the enthalpy change of the reaction. In the chemical reaction

$$CH_4(g) + 2O_2(g) \rightarrow CO_2(g) + 2H_2O(g)$$

the heat energy needed to break all the bonds in the reactants is 2736 kJ/mol. When the new bonds are formed in the products, the energy released is 3462 kJ/mol.

enthalpy change of reaction = (total energy needed to break bonds) − (total energy given out making bonds)

= .... − .... = ...

Now read the following paragraph and circle the correct options.

In the combustion of methane, 2736 kJ of heat energy per mole of methane is needed to **form / break** the **covalent / ionic** bonds in the reactants. The formation of the products **requires / releases** 3462 kJ of heat. This means that the heat energy **released / absorbed** by the reaction is **− / +** 726 kJ/mol. This reaction is **endothermic / exothermic**, given that more energy is released when the bonds are **formed / broken** than is **needed / used** when the bonds in the reactants are **formed / broken**.

6   a   The fact that bonds must be broken in the reactants before a chemical reaction can take place means that all reactions need a certain amount of energy to start. This energy is known as the **activation energy (E_a)** of the reaction (see Figure 7.3).

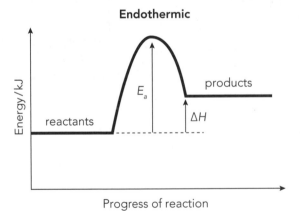

Figure 7.3: The reaction pathway diagram for a reaction showing the enthalpy change of reaction (ΔH) and the activation energy (E_a).

i Look closely at Figure 7.3 and give three key points that the reaction pathway diagram tells us about the energy changes involved in this reaction.

....

....

....

ii What would change if a similar reaction pathway diagram was drawn for an exothermic reaction?

....

....

....

b The following are definitions of important terms in this area of chemistry. Rearrange the words below to give the correct statement of the definition.

i **bond energy:**

break bond the energy one mole is of the energy needed to bonds

....

....

ii **heat of combustion:**

completely when the energy heat of combustion is substance the given out one mole of the burned is

....

....

....

iii **activation energy:**

energy minimum to place the energy is the reaction for needed take activation

....

....

....

Chapter 8

> Chapter 8

Rates of reaction

IN THIS CHAPTER YOU WILL:

Science skills:

- describe the different factors that affect the rate of a chemical reaction

- interpret graphs to show the different stages of a reaction and the factors that affect the rate of reaction.

English skills:

- learn the use of adjectives to express the differences between reactions

- consider the meaning of *effect* and *affect* in the context of reaction rate.

Exercise 8.1 Describing different reactions

IN THIS EXERCISE YOU WILL:

Science skills:

- describe several different chemical reactions that take place at different rates.

English skills:

- practise using adjectives to describe reactions more precisely.

LANGUAGE FOCUS

Adjectives are words that you can use to describe things, people, places, etc. Examples that you probably already know are *big*, *tall*, *long*, *important*, *interesting*.

In English, adjectives only have one form:

a <u>tall</u> boy; a <u>tall</u> girl

an <u>interesting</u> book; <u>interesting</u> books

Adjectives go in front of the thing they are describing or after *to be*:

It was an <u>important</u> experiment.

The experiment was <u>important</u>.

1   The following sentences describe different reactions. Rewrite the sentences, putting the adjective(s) given in the correct place.

   a   Hydrogen and oxygen take part in a reaction that can be used to power rockets. (*explosive*)

   ....

   ....

   b   Photosynthesis is a reaction that takes place in the leaves of plants. (*green*)

   ....

   ....

   c   Copper carbonate is coloured and is at room temperature but decomposes quickly when heated with a Bunsen burner, producing a powder. (*green / stable / black*)

   ....

   ....

   ....

   d   The metal zinc reacts with copper sulfate solution and the colour of the solution fades. (*blue*)

   ....

   ....

   e   The reaction between calcium carbonate and dilute hydrochloric acid produces a volume of gas. (*vigorous / large*)

   ....

   ....

Exercise 8.2 Factors affecting the rate of a reaction

IN THIS EXERCISE YOU WILL:

Science skills:

*   outline how factors such as concentration, pressure and the surface area of any solid affect the rate of a reaction.

English skills:

*   practise using terms that are involved in the discussion of rates of reaction.

KEY WORDS

reaction rate: a measure of how fast a reaction takes place

2 **a** The **reaction rate** is a measure of the speed with which the products are formed in a chemical reaction. Find and list 15 terms concerning reaction rate in the word search (13 are single words; two are two-word terms).

K	H	T	I	M	E	I	W	Z	K	V	S	I	R
R	C	T	N	E	X	P	L	O	S	I	V	E	E
S	R	O	E	M	J	P	L	X	R	Y	C	H	A
U	I	E	N	M	T	N	E	J	U	H	A	V	C
R	N	D	A	C	P	J	E	W	B	P	T	A	T
F	C	K	E	C	E	E	J	E	W	C	A	R	I
A	R	N	B	C	T	N	R	J	S	M	L	I	O
C	E	S	P	F	R	A	T	A	B	I	Y	A	N
E	A	O	R	A	U	E	N	R	T	O	S	B	R
A	S	E	O	S	Q	E	A	T	A	U	T	L	A
R	E	S	D	T	E	W	Y	S	Y	T	R	E	T
E	S	L	U	H	B	I	T	Z	E	J	I	E	E
A	I	O	C	T	T	Y	M	F	Y	S	S	O	F
A	S	W	T	P	R	E	S	S	U	R	E	F	N

....

....

....

....

....

b Use some of the words from the word search to complete the following passage. The rate of a chemical reaction is dependent on several factors:

• the c........................ of the reactants

• the s........................ a........................ of the particles of any solid reactants

• the p........................ of the reacting gases; in effect, this means their concentrations (see Figure 8.1)

• the t........................

• the presence of a c........................ (see Exercise 8.5).

All the factors discussed influence the reaction rate by affecting the frequency with which atoms or molecules collide (see Figure 8.1).

low pressure

high pressure

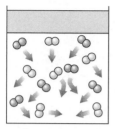
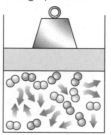

Collisions can occur between different molecules.

Collisions between different molecules are much more frequent.

Figure 8.1: Increasing the pressure of gases effectively increases the concentration of the gases and speeds up the reaction.

Exercise 8.3 Comparing different reactions

IN THIS EXERCISE YOU WILL:

Science skills:

- describe how factors such as concentration, pressure and the surface area of any solid affect the rate of a reaction.

- use the collision theory to explain the effect of the various factors on reaction rate.

English skills:

- use comparative adjectives and superlative adjectives.

KEY WORDS

collision theory: a theory which states that a chemical reaction takes place when particles of the reactants collide with sufficient energy to initiate the reaction

LANGUAGE FOCUS

Comparatives

Basic adjectives (*big, fast, complex*) are used to describe nouns, but to compare two nouns, you need comparative adjectives.

Adjectives with one syllable (*big, fast, small, …*) add *-er*:

big – bigger*   fast – faster   small – smaller

*adjectives ending *consonant–vowel–consonant* double the final consonant:

big – bigger   flat – flatter

Adjectives with two syllables, ending in *-y* or *-w*, add *-er*:

heavy – y → i – heavier   narrow – narrower

Other adjectives with two syllables or more add *more*:

complex – more complex   important – more important

Use *than* to connect the things being compared:

Rusting is a slow reaction. It is slower than burning.

If we increase the temperature, the reaction is faster than before.

Superlatives

Use superlative adjectives to compare several things and to express the 'most'.

Adjectives with *-er* comparative forms add *-est* to the basic adjective (*the biggest, the fastest, the heaviest, the narrowest*):

We tested the rate of reaction at 10, 20 and 30°C. The reaction was the slowest at 10°C.

Adjectives with *more* comparative forms add *most*:

the most complex, the most important

Three irregular adjectives

good – better – the best

bad – worse – the worst

far – further / farther – the furthest / farthest

3   As we think about the effects of changing reaction conditions, we will need to use comparative or superlative adjectives. Each part of this exercise includes sentences requiring comparative or superlative adjectives.

In parts **a** and **b**, underline the adjective in the first sentence. Then complete the sentences using the comparative and superlative forms of the adjective you have underlined. Use the example to help you.

Maira is investigating reaction rate. She measures how <u>fast</u> different solutions of hydrochloric acid react with marble chips. The 0.5 mol/dm³ solution reacted ....*faster*........ than the 0.2 mol/dm³ solution. The 1.0 mol/dm³ solution reacted ....*fastest*........ of all.

a   The difference in reaction rate is due to the difference in how concentrated the solutions are. The 0.5 mol/dm³ solution is .... than the 0.2 mol/dm³ solution. The 1.0 mol/dm³ solution is the...........................

b   Then, Maira wants to find the effect of high temperature on reaction rate. She investigates several temperatures .... than room temperature. The .... temperature she investigates is 80 °C.

Complete the following sentences using the correct comparative or superlative adjectives.

c   Next, Maira investigates the effect of the size of the marble chips using the same mass each time. She gradually decreases the size of the pieces she uses. She performs her first reaction with the .... marble chips. Then she performs the reaction with medium-sized marble chips. Finally, the .... particle size she uses is marble powder.

The marble chips in the first reaction have the .... surface area.

The surface area of the chips in the second reaction is ....

However, the marble powder has the .... surface area of all.

4   The following statements are comparisons related to the factors that affect the rate of a chemical reaction. Some use the **collision theory** to help explain the result of the experiment. Read the statements and circle the correct options.

a   An experiment was performed to find how the surface area of a solid affects the rate of reaction. Hydrochloric acid was added to powdered marble chips. One powder was made up of large pieces, the other of small pieces. The same mass of powder was used in each experiment. The rate of reaction was **faster / fastest / slower** when more powdered marble was used. The **fastest / slower / slowest** reaction of the two occurred when the large pieces of marble chips were used.

b   When concentrated solutions are used in an experiment, there are more particles present in the volume of solution used. This means that there is a **lower / greater** chance of the particles colliding and reacting with each other. As a result, the rate of reaction **increases / decreases** with increased concentration of the solutions.

c   The rate of reaction between two gases is studied at two different pressures. The amount of each gas is the same in both cases. This means that the gases at the higher pressure are in a **smaller / larger** volume. The molecules must be **closer / further apart** at the higher pressure. This means that the molecules will probably collide and react with each other **more / less** often. Increasing the pressure on a gas mixture **decreases / increases** the rate of reaction.

LANGUAGE TIP

When making comparisons, the opposite of *more* is *less*, and the opposite of *the most* is *the least*. Therefore, *it is <u>less complex</u>* means something similar to *it is <u>simpler</u>*, and *<u>the most</u> concentrated* is *<u>the least</u> dilute*. *Less* and *least* are used less frequently than *more* and *most*.

d If the temperature of a reacting mixture is increased, the particles will have more kinetic energy. This affects the rate of reaction for two reasons.

- The particles are moving **slower / faster** and so will collide with each other **more / less** often.

- When they collide, there is a **higher / lower** chance of the particles having energy greater than the minimum (the activation energy) needed for reaction. More collisions will produce a faster reaction.

Exercise 8.4 Interpreting graphs on reaction rate

IN THIS EXERCISE YOU WILL:

Science skills:

- describe how graphs can be used to show how the rate of a reaction changes with time.

English skills:

- practise the key terms used when drawing and interpreting graphs.

KEY WORDS

dependent variable: the variable that is measured during a scientific investigation

independent variable: the variable that is altered during a scientific investigation

LANGUAGE FOCUS

When you study chemistry, knowing how to express the key features of a graph and how to talk about your interpretation of graphs are very important skills. This means you will need to learn the key language for talking about graphs, such as 'best-fit line' or 'gradient'.

When studying the rate of a reaction it is useful to <u>plot a graph</u> of the results.

When drawing a graph we use vertical and horizontal <u>axes</u> to plot our results.

Time is the usual variable we plot along the horizontal <u>x-axis</u> of the graph for a rate experiment.

When we have plotted the points of a graph, we then draw a <u>curve</u> through them.

The curve we draw through the points of a graph should be a <u>best-fit line</u> that shows the trend of the data.

The <u>gradient</u> (or <u>slope</u>) of the curve at a given time shows the rate of reaction at that time.

CONTINUED

Time is the usual __independent variable__ we plot along the horizontal x-axis of the graph for a rate experiment. The __dependent variable__ is plotted on the vertical y-axis.

To help you learn these terms quickly, make word-cards with words and phrases like 'plot a graph' and keep them in your pocket to test yourself in free moments. You can also label all the graphs you can find in your coursebooks and/or in your notes.

5 a Find 19 terms commonly used to describe and interpret graphs in the word strings. Then use the terms to complete the table. The first word has been done for you.

horizontalaxisorigincurveslopechangepointsplateaugradient dependentvariabletangent

pointflattensouttrendbestfitlinestraightlineoutliermeasure independentvariableverticalaxis

Terms	Definition
horizontal axis	The x-axis of the graph; the axis along which the .... (the variable you ....) is plotted
....	The y-axis of the graph; the axis along which the .... variable (the variable you ....) is plotted
outlier	An anomalous .... that does not fit close to the .... or .... of the graph; the line of the graph should not include this point
....	The point 0,0 of the graph
The .... or .... of the graph	The rate of change shown by the graph; the steepness of the curve shows how quickly the reaction is taking place
....	A straight line drawn at a point on the curve of the graph, used to work out the rate of reaction at that time
....	The line drawn that passes through or close to as many .... as possible; this can show the overall .... in the results
plateau	Part of the graph where the curve ...., showing no further reaction

b The graph in Figure 8.2 shows how the rate of a reaction changes with time. Read the following description of region **A**. The first part of the description discusses the gradient. Then the description discusses how much product is being formed in a period of time and the rate of reaction.

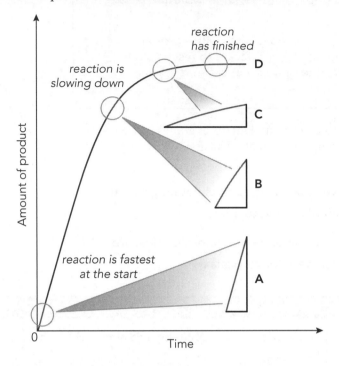

Figure 8.2: How the rate of a reaction changes with time.

At **A**, the gradient is at its greatest. This shows that a large amount of product is formed in a short time. The reaction is fastest here.

Using the description for region **A** as an example, complete the following statements for regions **B–D**.

i At **B**, the gradient ....

This shows that ....

The reaction is slower here.

ii At **C**, the gradient is very small. This shows that only

....

The reaction is ....

iii At **D**, the graph has flattened. This shows that no more product is being

formed. The reaction ....

LANGUAGE TIP

Use the linker *as* to express the idea 'progressively', 'while the process happens':

It shows the changes __as__ the reaction takes place.

They change __as__ time passes.

Exercise 8.5 Catalysts

IN THIS EXERCISE YOU WILL:

Science skills:

- define a catalyst and describe the effect of a catalyst on a reaction.

English skills:

- consider the difference between *affect* (verb) and *effect* (noun), and learn how to use them.

KEY WORDS

catalyst: a substance that increases the rate of a chemical reaction but itself remains unchanged at the end of the reaction

enzymes: protein molecules that act as biological catalysts

LANGUAGE FOCUS

In this chapter, the words *affect* and *effect* are often used. It is important to remember the difference between the two. In this context *affect* is a verb and *effect* is a noun. The *effect* is what is produced when a reaction is *affected* by a change in conditions.

The <u>effect</u> of increasing the temperature is that the reaction goes faster.

Increasing the temperature <u>affects</u> the reaction in a way that speeds it up.

6   Complete the following statements about the different results of changing conditions on the rate of a chemical reaction. Use the words below (some may be needed more than once, others not at all).

affect   affects   effect   effects

a   The .... of raising the temperature or the pressure of a reaction

between gases are the same. The reaction speeds up.

b   Reducing the particle size of a solid in a reaction .... the rate by

speeding it up.

c   Adding a **catalyst** to a reaction has the .... of increasing the rate

of reaction.

d   Although a catalyst .... a reaction by speeding it up, there is no

.... on the amount of catalyst itself at the end of the reaction.

The catalyst is not used up in the reaction.

7 The rate of some reactions can be affected by adding a catalyst.

    a Review what the **affect / effect** of a catalyst is (circle the correct word). Then reorder the following sentence parts **i–v** to give the definition of a catalyst. Write the full definition in the space provided.

        i … without being used up during the reaction.

        ii The catalyst is chemically unchanged at …

        iii … speeds up the rate of a chemical reaction …

        iv A catalyst is a substance that …

        v … the end of the reaction.

        ....

        ....

        ....

        ....

        ....

        ....

    b Complete the following paragraph by circling the correct word in each case.

        Enzymes are proteins that are **biological / physical** examples of **catalysts / catalases**. This means that enzymes **affect / effect** reactions in living cells to make them go **faster / slower**. Catalysts and enzymes are important because they help make reactions occur at much **milder / more hostile** conditions than would be needed **with / without** them.

Chapter 9

Reversible reactions and equilibrium

Science skills:

- describe how certain chemical reactions such as the dehydration of certain crystals can be reversed

- understand that some reversible reactions can reach equilibrium in a closed system, and that the physical conditions can affect the position of an equilibrium.

English skills:

- develop confidence in using vocabulary and ideas involved in describing the Haber process

- use modal verbs to make predictions and draw conclusions about the effects of changing conditions on reversible reactions.

Exercise 9.1 Reversible reactions

N THIS EXERCISE YOU WILL:

Science skills:

- investigate the basics of reversible reactions.

English skills:

- practise working out the meanings of scientific terms by looking at prefixes, suffixes and roots.

KEY WORDS

dehydration: a chemical reaction in which water is removed from a compound

hydrated salts: salts whose crystals contain combined water (*water of crystallisation*) as part of the structure

> **LANGUAGE FOCUS**
>
> In science, you can often work out the meaning of a term from its parts.
>
> A suffix tells you the kind of word it is.
>
> Words ending in -*ation* are nouns and often refer to processes,
> e.g. *separation*, *saturation*, *oxidation*. They are frequently from verbs ending
> in -*ate* which also express process or change, e.g. *separate*, *saturate*.
>
> Words ending in -*ous* are adjectives. They describe a state or a
> fixed characteristic:
>
> *a generous person*   *a ridiculous idea*   *a porous solid*
>
> Words that end in -*ed* are often adjectives. They describe reactions or results
> of processes:
>
> *I'm interested* = my reaction   *a saturated solution* = a result of saturation
>
> A prefix tells you about meaning. For example, *an-* and *de-* mean 'without'
> but they are slightly different.
>
> - *An-* expresses a fixed state; it does not express change or process,
>   e.g. *anacidic* – without acid, *anangular* – without angles.
>
> - *De-* expresses a process of taking away. The result of the process is 'being
>   without', e.g. *deacidify* – take away the acidity, *detoxify* – take away
>   the toxin.
>
> The root of the word can be part of a family. Two of the words above are in
> the *acid* family. Some word families are related, such as the *water* families.
> In Ancient Greek, *water* was *hudor* and in Latin, it was *aqua*, so English words
> with *hydro/a* and with *aqu-* are from related families.

1   a   Read the Language Focus box carefully, then match the words to their
        meanings in the following grid by drawing lines.

anhydrous	making something absorb water (n)
aqueous	dried (water has been lost or removed)
dehydrated	making something lose water (n)
hydration	containing no water (adj)
dehydration	made of or containing water (adj)

    b   The raindrop in Figure 9.1 contains words related to simple decomposition
        reactions, particularly involving loss of water. Complete the passage using the
        words given (some words may be used more than once).

Figure 9.1: 'Raindrop' word cloud relating to some thermal decomposition reactions.

anhydrous   decomposes   decomposition   dehydrated

dehydration   reverse   simpler   split up

Thermal .... is a type of chemical reaction in which a compound is .... into .... substances. For example, zinc carbonate .... as shown in the following word equation.

zinc carbonate → zinc oxide + carbon dioxide

Usually, this reaction is carried out in an open tube and the gas produced escapes into the air. It is difficult to .... this experiment.

However, if we can collect both products, there are some reactions which can be reversed, if the products are put back together. An example of this is the .... of copper(II) sulfate crystals ($CuSO_4 \cdot 5H_2O$).

$$CuSO_4 \cdot 5H_2O(s) \xrightarrow{\text{heat}} CuSO_4(s) + 5H_2O(g)$$
light blue crystals   white powder

In this case, the reaction results in a colour change from blue to white. The physical structure of the crystals is also destroyed. The water removed can be condensed separately (see Figure 9.2).

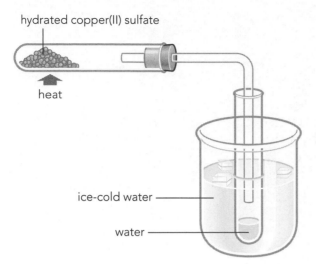

Figure 9.2: The dehydration of copper sulfate crystals.

The white .... copper(II) sulfate and the water are cooled down. Then the dehydration reaction can be reversed by slowly adding the water back to the white .... powder. The .... reaction is strongly exothermic and the colour of the powder returns to blue.

c   Other **hydrated salts** can take part in dehydration reactions that can be reversed. Complete the description using the participles of the verbs in brackets.

Several different hydrated salts can be .... (*dehydrate*) in a similar way to copper(II) sulfate. Examples of such salts are cobalt(II) chloride and iron(II) sulfate. When these salts are .... (*crystallise*) they have a defined amount of water chemically combined in their crystals. Hydrated cobalt(II) chloride is a pink crystalline salt. When heated it is dehydrated to a form which is blue. The reaction is endothermic.

$$CoCl_2 \cdot 6H_2O \xrightarrow{\text{heat}} CoCl_2 + 6H_2O$$
$$\text{pink} \qquad\qquad \text{blue}$$

The reverse of this reaction can be .... (*carry out*) using the anhydrous form of the salt. When water is .... (*add*) to blue anhydrous cobalt(II) chloride, it turns pink. The dehydration of cobalt(II) chloride can easily be .... (*reverse*). These two reactions can be .... (*combine*) into one equation using the ⇌ sign.

$$CoCl_2 \cdot 6H_2O \rightleftharpoons CoCl_2 + 6H_2O$$
$$\text{pink} \qquad\qquad \text{blue}$$

These dehydration reactions involving a colour change are .... (*use*) as a test for the presence of water.

LANGUAGE TIP

Remember the *-ed* part of verbs can be adjectives, but they can also be participles and used in passive sentences:

We use concentrated salt solutions to prepare crystals. (= adjective)

The solutions were concentrated by carefully evaporating off much of the water. (= participle)

Exercise 9.2 The Haber process and fertiliser production

KEY WORD

fertiliser: a substance added to the soil to replace essential elements lost when crops are harvested, which enables crops to grow faster and increases the yield

Haber process: the industrial manufacture of ammonia by the reaction of nitrogen with hydrogen in the presence of an iron catalyst

reversible reaction: a chemical reaction that can go either forwards or backwards, depending on the conditions

2 **a** The **Haber process**, by which nitrogen and hydrogen are reacted together to make ammonia, is the basis of the modern **fertiliser** industry:

nitrogen + hydrogen $\rightleftharpoons$ ammonia

$$N_2 + 3H_2 \rightleftharpoons 2NH_3$$

Figure 9.3 shows a flow diagram of the stages of the Haber process. The different steps are lettered **A–H**, with **G**, **E** and **B** representing the conditions in the reaction vessel (**H**).

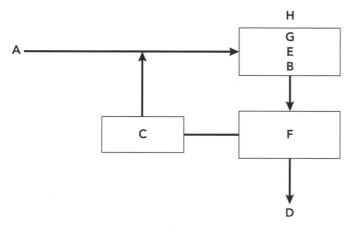

Figure 9.3: The stages of the Haber process.

Match the labels in the table to the letters in Figure 9.3, and write each letter in the table. One has been completed for you.

Label	Position on diagram
reaction vessel	
condenser	
iron catalyst	
liquid ammonia	
recycled nitrogen and hydrogen gases	
temperature of about 450 °C	G
mixture of nitrogen and hydrogen gases enters	
pressure of 20 000 kPa	

b   A large amount of ammonia produced by the Haber process is used to make fertilisers such as ammonium nitrate. To do this, the ammonia is reacted with nitric acid. This is a neutralisation reaction.

ammonia + nitric acid ⇌ ammonium nitrate

$$NH_3 + HNO_3 \rightleftharpoons NH_4NO_3$$

Statements **S–Z** list the stages involved in making ammonia and converting it into ammonium nitrate.

i   Complete the statements using the words below.

compressed   recycled   nitrogen   ammonia

condensed   hydrogen   iron catalyst

S   Hydrogen is made from natural gas, and .... is separated from the air.

T   An .... is used to increase the rate of reaction.

U   The mixture of gases is .... at a high temperature in a reaction vessel.

V   The hydrogen and nitrogen are mixed in a ratio of 3:1.

W   The ammonia formed is ....

X   Any unreacted nitrogen and hydrogen is ....

Y   The .... is reacted with nitric acid to form ammonium nitrate.

Z   The nitrogen and .... react to produce ammonia.

ii Statements **S–Z** are not in the correct order. Reorder the steps using information from stages **a** and **b** of this question, and write the letters in the grid. Two have been entered for you.

1	2	3	4	5	6	7	8
S							Y

3 The key reaction of the Haber process is a **reversible reaction**.

$$N_2 + 3H_2 \rightleftharpoons 2NH_3$$

In a closed system, where nothing is added to or removed from the reaction mixture, a dynamic equilibrium is reached.

Match the terms or ideas to their meanings and complete the answer grid underneath the table. Two connections have been entered already.

	Key term or idea		Definition
1	a reversible reaction	A	a reaction that takes place in both directions
2	a dynamic equilibrium	B	$2NH_3 \rightarrow N_2 + 3H_2$
3	a closed system	C	the concentrations of substances present at equilibrium
4	the forward reaction in the Haber process	D	a reaction mixture in which both the forward and the backward reaction are happening at the same rate
5	symbol for a reversible reaction	E	$\rightleftharpoons$
6	the backward reaction in the Haber process	F	a system where nothing is added or removed
7	the equilibrium position	G	$N_2 + 3H_2 \rightarrow 2NH_3$

1	2	3	4	5	6	7
A						C

Exercise 9.3 Factors affecting the amount of product formed by a reversible reaction

IN THIS EXERCISE YOU WILL:

Science skills:

- understand how various factors affect the position of equilibrium for a reversible reaction.

English skills:

- use modal verbs to make predictions about how various factors affect the equilibrium position.

LANGUAGE FOCUS

In making predictions and conclusions about reactions, we often need to use phrases such as *we should see*, *the metal will react* and *this substance could act as a catalyst*. These phrases all use modal verbs, which include: *could*, *should*, *may*, *might* and *will*:

could / may / might = you think it's possible

will / will not = you are sure the thing is going to happen (or not)

may not / might not = you think it possibly won't happen (Note: *could not* is not used in this context)

should / should not = if we didn't make a mistake / if everything works, it will / will not happen

Modal verbs are used with a second verb to form a sentence or question:

It *might work*.

That *should* not *happen*, if you do it correctly.

You do not need to use *don't* to form the negative; just add *not*.

You cannot use two modal verbs together:

~~It will should hydrate the salt.~~ → It should hydrate the salt.

~~The acid could should neutralise the alkali.~~ → The acid should neutralise the alkali.

4   The concentrations of reactants and products in an equilibrium mixture (the equilibrium position) are changed only if certain conditions are changed. Because we have observations on many reversible reactions, we can make predictions and draw conclusions about the effects of changing conditions on the amount of product formed by a reaction.

Read the following sentences and circle the correct modal verb.

a   Because the Haber process uses a reaction between gases, the amount of product formed **might / will not** be affected by changes in pressure.

b   Lowering the pressure in a reaction between gases **should / should not** *produce* an effect on the equilibrium position, if the products have a greater or lower volume than the reactants.

c   In general, an increase in pressure **might / will** move the equilibrium position to the side of the reaction that has the smaller number of moles. That side **will / may** occupy a smaller volume.

d   Increasing the temperature of an equilibrium mixture **might / will** *produce* an effect which depends on whether the forward reaction is exothermic or endothermic.

e   A change in temperature **may not / will** affect the equilibrium position of a reaction mixture.

f   A catalyst speeds up both the forward and backward reactions in an equilibrium mixture. Therefore, a catalyst **may / will** have no effect on the proportion of product at equilibrium.

5   **a**   The Haber process involves a reaction between two gases. The amount of ammonia produced is affected by the pressure at which the reaction is carried out (see Figure 9.4).

$$N_2(g) + 3H_2(g) \rightleftharpoons 2NH_3(g)$$

4 moles of gas   2 moles of gas

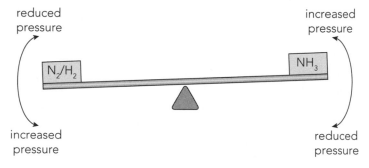

Figure 9.4: The effect of pressure on the Haber process.

Complete the statement about the effect of reducing the pressure. Include modal verbs.

In general, a decrease in pressure ....

....

....

b   In general, an increase in temperature will move an equilibrium position in the direction of the endothermic reaction. The reaction from the Haber process can be used to show this effect.

exothermic →

$$N_2 + 3H_2 \rightleftharpoons 2NH_3$$

← endothermic

In this case the forward reaction is exothermic. The backward reaction is endothermic.

If the temperature is increased there will be less ammonia in the equilibrium mixture (see Figure 9.5).

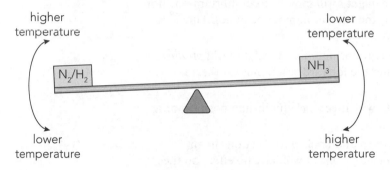

Figure 9.5: The effect of temperature on the Haber process.

Complete the following statement about the effect of a decrease in temperature on the amount of ammonia produced. Include modal verbs.

In general, a decrease in temperature ....

....

....

Oxidation and reduction

Exercise 10.1 Oxidation and reduction

1   Figure 10.1 shows how copper can be made from copper(II) oxide in the laboratory.

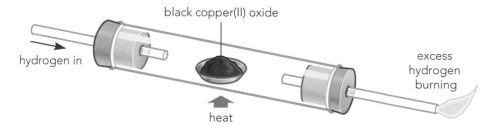

Figure 10.1: The **reduction** of copper(II) oxide by hydrogen.

Hydrogen removes oxygen from the copper(II) oxide to form water vapour (see Figure 10.2). The colour of the powder changes from black to the characteristic colour of copper.

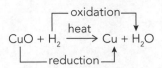

Figure 10.2: The equation for the reduction of copper.

We say that the copper(II) oxide has been *reduced*, because it has lost oxygen. The hydrogen has gained oxygen. Hydrogen has been *oxidised*.

a Complete the following two general statements:

If a substance *gains oxygen* in a reaction, it is said to be ....

If a substance *loses oxygen* in a reaction, it is said to be ....

b In the reaction in Figure 10.1 the reduction of copper(II) oxide has been caused by hydrogen. It is said to be a reducing agent. Read the definition of a reducing agent below, then write a similar definition for an oxidising agent. You can use a form of the verbs *add* or *give* in your definition.

A *reducing agent* is an element or compound that will remove oxygen from a compound.

An *oxidising agent* ....

....

> **LANGUAGE TIP**
>
> When scientists explain a chemical term, they often use the structure *If..., it is said to be...*:
>
> *If carbon monoxide gains oxygen to form CO$_2$ when it burns, the carbon monoxide is said to be oxidised.*

2 In industry, the blast furnace reaction is used to extract iron from iron oxide. The reduction of iron ore (haematite) is economically very important. Carbon monoxide is the reducing agent in this case.

Complete the word equation by writing the products on the lines indicated by the arrows. Label the word equation by writing the words *reduction* and **oxidation** in the correct boxes.

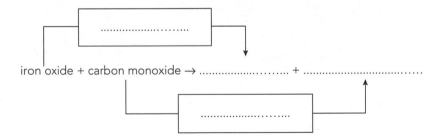

Since both **red**uction and **ox**idation must take place within the same reaction, the term '**redox reaction**' is often used when describing these reactions.

Exercise 10.2 Further definitions of oxidation and reduction

IN THIS EXERCISE YOU WILL:

Science skills:

- investigate other definitions of oxidation and reduction in terms of the loss or gain of electrons.

English skills:

- practise writing definitions related to oxidation and reduction.

KEY WORDS

oxidising agent: a substance which oxidises another substance during a redox reaction

reducing agent: a substance which reduces another substance during a redox reaction

LANGUAGE FOCUS

Define is an important command word. *Define* means you must give a short, precise meaning of the term given. Definitions often use *which* or *that* to link the parts of the definition together:

A **reducing agent** is a substance <u>that</u> will remove oxygen from a compound during a chemical reaction.

Carbon monoxide is a reducing agent <u>which</u> is used to extract iron from iron ore.

Note the pattern (X) is a (Y) that/which + verb. The pattern can also be (X) is a (Y) that/which + subject + verb:

Carbon monoxide is a reducing agent <u>which</u> industry uses to extract iron from iron ore.

3   One way to define oxidation and reduction is to consider whether oxygen has been gained or lost in a reaction. Other definitions have been introduced, based on whether electrons have been gained or lost from an atom, molecule or ion during a reaction.

Complete the following alternative definitions of oxidation and reduction. These definitions are the reverse of those involving oxygen and complete the useful memory aid (OIL RIG) shown in Figure 10.3.

OIL-RIG

Oxidation **I**s …
Reduction **I**s …

Figure 10.3: A memory aid for defining oxidation and reduction.

a Oxidation is

....

b Reduction is

....

Now complete the following definitions based on this new understanding of the processes involved.

c An **oxidising agent** is

....

....

d A reducing agent is

....

....

Exercise 10.3 Redox and the transfer of electrons

IN THIS EXERCISE YOU WILL:

Science skills:

- extend the idea of a redox reaction to include the definition in terms of electron gain or loss.

English skills:

- look at the differences between the command words *state*, *give*, *sketch* and *discuss*.

KEY WORDS

oxidation number: a number given to show whether an element has been oxidised or reduced; the oxidation number of a simple ion is simply the charge on the ion

LANGUAGE TIP

The word *agent* is often used in technical contexts to refer to the thing or person that makes something happen:

When you want to reduce copper(II) oxide to copper metal, you need a reducing <u>agent,</u> such as carbon.

4 The most important of the extended ideas of a redox reaction defines oxidation and reduction in terms of the loss or gain of electrons.

The reaction between chlorine and potassium iodide solution is a displacement reaction. Chlorine displaces iodine from potassium iodide.

LANGUAGE FOCUS

State, give, sketch and *discuss* are important command words.

State is a scientific word that means to express facts in clear terms, for instance to say how something always happens or what something is:

<u>*State*</u> *whether oxidation involves the gain or loss of electrons during a redox reaction.*

Give is often used with a paragraph of text to mean find or remember an answer, and then write it:

<u>*Give*</u> *the names of two of the most frequently used reducing agents in chemistry.*

Sketch is used when asking for a simple drawing of a process showing the key features (often used in conjunction with 'label' or 'labelled' when the parts of a drawing need some description):

<u>*Sketch*</u> *a labelled diagram of the apparatus used to filter off the crystals after preparing a salt.*

Discuss is a scientific word meaning to write about or talk about issue(s) or topic(s) in-depth in a structured way. Here you will need to write or talk about different options and suggest a final answer. There may not necessarily be one final correct answer to the question:

<u>*Discuss*</u> *the merits of the different definitions of oxidation and reduction.*

Discuss the changes taking place in this reaction. In each case, state whether electrons are gained or lost, and whether each change is oxidation or reduction.

a Chlorine molecules split up into atoms and then become chloride negative ions.

This is ....

b Iodide ions become iodine atoms and then form iodine molecules.

This is ....

c Label the word equation (the halogen displacement reaction of chlorine with potassium iodide) by writing *reduction* and *oxidation* in the correct boxes.

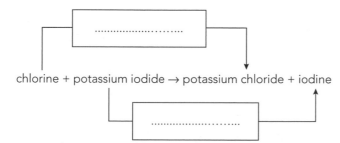

5   When metal atoms form ions they lose electrons to become positive ions.
    The metal atoms are oxidised. This degree of oxidation is shown by the **oxidation
    number** of the metal in that compound. For example, in copper(II) oxide, copper
    has an oxidation number of +2 and is present as the Cu^{2+} ion.

    Give the oxidation numbers of the metals present in the compounds listed in the
    table, then give the formula of the positive ion present in each case.

Compound	Oxidation number of metal present	Formula of metal ion present
copper(II) sulfate		
iron(III) oxide		
cobalt(II) chloride		
copper(I) oxide		

Exercise 10.4 Redox reactions

IN THIS EXERCISE YOU WILL:

Science skills:

•   explain how redox reactions are used in the extraction of metals.

English skills:

•   look at the use of *explain* as a command word.

6   Iron is produced in the blast furnace by the reduction of iron ore by carbon.
    Aluminium is more reactive than iron and so must be produced by reduction
    of its ore during electrolysis. The aluminium ions (Al^{3+}) gain electrons during
    electrolysis to produce the metal.

Explain is another important command word. *Explain* means to make the relationships between things evident, so you should say both what happens in a process and why or how it happens.

Explain why the extraction of iron in the blast furnace is often referred to as the reduction of iron ore.

Useful expressions to help you explain a process are:

This is because…,   That is why…,   The reason for this is… …and so…:

The reason for this is that iron is the most important product from the furnace and so the removal of oxygen from the ore is the most important reaction taking place.

This is because iron is the most important product from the furnace and so we describe the process by the reaction in which oxygen is removed from the iron ore.

a   Explain why the reaction taking place in the blast furnace is actually a redox reaction and not just a reduction of the iron ore.

....

....

....

....

b   Explain why the conversion of aluminium ions to aluminium metal atoms is a reduction reaction.

....

....

....

> Chapter 11
Acids and bases

IN THIS CHAPTER YOU WILL:

Science skills:

- look at the differences between acids and bases, including those bases that are soluble in water (the alkalis)

- describe how to distinguish between acids and alkalis using indicators, and understand the pH scale.

English skills:

- investigate some of the language used to describe acid and alkali solutions, including use of the terms *dilute* and *concentrated*

- consider the meaning of the terms *weak* and *strong* when used for acids.

Exercise 11.1 Acids, bases and neutralisation

IN THIS EXERCISE YOU WILL:

Science skills:

- be introduced to some of the main ideas about what acids and bases are and the characteristic reactions they take part in.

English skills:

- practise the language that distinguishes acids, bases and alkalis from each other.

KEY WORDS

acid: a substance that dissolves in water, producing $H^+(aq)$ ions – a solution of an acid turns litmus red and has a pH below 7
Acids act as proton donors

alkalis: soluble bases that produce $OH^-(aq)$ ions in water – a solution of an alkali turns litmus blue and has a pH above 7

base: a substance that neutralises an acid, producing a salt and water as the only products; bases act as proton acceptors

1   There are several different ways of defining an **acid**. Some are based on simple observation. Others contain an explanation of what is happening in an acid solution. Separate the words in the following word strings to form sentences. Then write the sentences on the lines provided. An example has been done for you.

Anacidisasubstancethatturnsmoistlitmuspaperred.

An acid is a substance that turns moist litmus paper red.

a AnacidisasubstancethatgivesasolutionwithapHlessthan7whendissolvedinwater.

....

....

b Anacidisasolutionthatreactswithanalkalitogiveasaltandwateronly.

....

....

c Anaciddissolvesinwatertogiveasolutionthatcontainsanexcessofhydrogenions.

....

....

2 **Bases** are the chemical opposites of acids. They neutralise acids to give salts. Look at the Venn diagram in Figure 11.1.

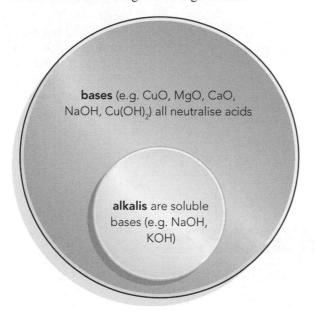

Figure 11.1: Venn diagram showing the relationship between bases and **alkalis**.

Write four bullet points about what the Venn diagram tells you about bases.

- ....

- ....

- ....

- ....

> **LANGUAGE TIP**
>
> To express quantity, you can use *all* in front of the noun: <u>*All*</u> *gases,* <u>*all*</u> *information.* You can also use *Not all* or *Some,* and *No:*
>
> <u>*Not all*</u> *scientists are chemists;* <u>*some*</u> *scientists are biologists.*
>
> *There is* <u>*no*</u> *hydrogen in the Earth's atmosphere.*

3   Complete the following statements using the words below. You may need to use some words more than once. Refer to questions **1** and **2** to help you.

dissolve   **excess**   **higher**   **hydroxides**   **insoluble**

ions   **lower**   **neutralised**   **only**   **red**

Acids:

*   are solutions containing an excess of H^+ .... and have a pH .... than 7.0

*   turn blue litmus ....

*   are .... by a base to give a salt and water ....

Bases:

*   are the oxides and .... of metals

*   neutralise acids to give a salt and water only

*   are mainly .... in water.

Alkalis:

*   are bases that .... in water, and feel soapy to the skin

*   give solutions containing an .... of OH^-........................

*   give solutions with a pH .... than 7.0 and turn .... litmus blue.

> **LANGUAGE TIP**
>
> It's important to remember that bases and alkalis are the chemical opposites of acids. The family of bases includes alkalis, but alkalis are soluble in water.

Exercise 11.2 The pH scale and indicators

IN THIS EXERCISE YOU WILL:

Science skills:

*   investigate ideas behind the pH scale and the use of indicators.

English skills:

*   learn how to use adjectives when making comparisons about acids and alkalis.

KEY WORDS

indicator: a substance which changes colour when added to acidic or alkaline solutions, e.g. litmus or thymolphthalein

pH scale: a scale running from below 0 to 14, used for expressing the acidity or alkalinity of a solution; a neutral solution has a pH of 7

universal indicator: a mixture of indicators that has different colours in solutions of different pH

An **indicator** is a substance that changes colour at different pH values. Solutions are acidic because of the presence of an excess of hydrogen ions and pH measures this. Indicators have this name due to their ability to indicate the pH of a solution.

Universal indicator is a mixture of indicators. It can produce a whole range of colours depending on the pH of the solution being tested (see Figure 11.2).

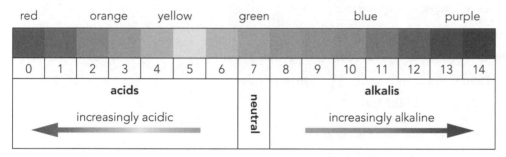

Figure 11.2: The **pH scale** and universal indicator colours.

LANGUAGE FOCUS

When you compare solutions, you often need to use the adjectives *acidic* and *alkaline* and the following comparison words: *more… (than), less… (than), the most, the least.*

For example, to compare two solutions use *more* or *less*:

A solution with a pH of 2.0 is <u>more acidic</u> than one with a pH of 6.0.

A solution of pH 10.0 is <u>less alkaline</u> than one of pH 13.0.

To compare more than two solutions and identify the solution with the highest or lowest acidity or alkalinity, use *the most* or *the least*:

For three acid solutions with pH values of 1.0, 4.0 and 6.5 the following is true:

The acid solution with pH 1.0 is <u>the most acidic</u>.

The solution with pH 6.5 is <u>the least acidic</u>.

CONTINUED

You may also want to compare solutions by how *dilute* or *concentrated* a solution is. For the same acid or alkali, this can be linked directly to the pH of the solution. Use *more*, *less*, *the most* and *the least* in front of the adjective:

A 0.5 mol/dm³ solution of hydrochloric acid is <u>more concentrated</u> *than a 0.1 mol/dm³ solution of the same acid.*

A sodium hydroxide solution of pH 13 must be <u>less dilute</u> *than one of pH 10, as it has the higher pH.*

Of three solutions of nitric acid with pH values of 1.0, 2.0 and 3.0, the solution with pH 3.0 must be <u>the least concentrated</u>. *The nitric acid solution with pH 1.0 must be* <u>the most concentrated</u>.

---

4   Read the Language Focus box carefully. Then complete the following paragraphs using the correct comparatives or letters, as appropriate.

Ashraf made three solutions of nitric acid and tested them with a pH meter. The values were found to be **A** = pH 2.0, **B** = pH 6.0 and **C** = pH 4.0. These results mean that solutions **B** and **C** are .... than solution **A**. Solution **B** is .... of the three.

Ashraf placed the solutions in order of increasing acidity:

.... < .... < ....

Since these are solutions of the same acid, the pH values must mean that solution **B** is ....concentrated of the three.

Zuleika was given three solutions of sodium hydroxide, labelled **X**, **Y** and **Z**. Two of these (**Y** and **Z**) were found to have the same pH: 9.0 using the pH meter. Solution **X** had a pH of 13.0. These results mean that solution **X** is .... than the other solutions. Solutions **Y** and **Z** have the same pH and they have .... alkalinity.

Placing the solutions in order of decreasing alkalinity gives:

.... > .... = ...

As they are all sodium hydroxide solutions, solution **X** must be .... than the other two.

Exercise 11.3 Strong and weak acids

IN THIS EXERCISE YOU WILL:

Science skills:

- investigate the distinction between strong and weak acids.

English skills:

- look at the importance of the terms *strong* and *weak* when describing acids.

KEY WORDS

strong acid: an acid that is completely ionised when dissolved in water – this produces the highest possible concentration of $H^+(aq)$ ions in solution, e.g. hydrochloric acid

weak acid: an acid that is only partially dissociated into ions in water – usually this produces a low concentration of $H^+(aq)$ in the solution, e.g. ethanoic acid

Vinegar, lemon juice and spoilt milk are all sour tasting because of the presence of acids. The acids present in these substances are all **weak acids**.

When describing acids and alkalis, the terms *strong* and *weak* have very specific meanings. **Strong acids** are completely dissociated into ions in water whereas weak acids such as ethanoic acid are only partly split into ions when dissolved. In aqueous solution, most of the ethanoic acid molecules remain intact. This means that the concentration of hydrogen ions is less than expected in this solution of a weak acid, and the solution is less acidic.

LANGUAGE FOCUS

It is important to remember that, in the context of acids and alkalis, the terms *weak* and *strong* do not mean the same thing as *concentrated* and *dilute*.

Weak/strong refers to how dissociated (split up) into ions the acid molecules are when dissolved in water.

A *weak* acid is an acid which is only partially split into ions in solution in water.

A *strong* acid, such as hydrochloric or nitric acid, is completely dissociated into ions in solution.

However, the terms *concentrated* and *dilute* refer to the amount of water added to an acid or alkali to make a solution.

When you see *more acidic / less acidic* it refers to the pH of the solution (the concentration of hydrogen ions present). In the same way, *more alkaline / less alkaline* refers to the concentration of hydroxide ions present (as shown by the pH of the solution).

5 Complete the following statements about strong acids and weak acids by circling the correct word of the alternatives given.

Hydrochloric acid is a **weak / strong** acid. Hydrogen chloride gas consists of **covalent / ionic** molecules. When they dissolve in water these molecules **partly / completely** split up into hydrogen and **chlorine / chloride** ions, producing as many hydrogen ions in the solution as possible.

Ethanoic acid is a **weak / strong** acid. When it dissolves in water **some / all** of the molecules dissociate (split) into ions. The majority of the molecules remain intact. This means that the concentration of hydrogen ions is **more / less** than it could be if all the molecules had split into ions.

Mary makes solutions of hydrochloric acid and ethanoic acid that have the same concentration. The hydrochloric acid solution will have the **higher / lower** pH value. It has the **higher / lower** concentration of hydrogen ions and is the **more / less** acidic solution.

6 Read the following statements and say whether they are True or False. Assume that all the acid solutions are of the same concentration.

Statement	True / False
A sulfuric acid solution is less corrosive than a solution of ethanoic acid.	
A hydrochloric acid solution will conduct electricity better than an ethanoic acid solution.	
An ethanoic acid solution will produce carbon dioxide gas at a faster rate than a hydrochloric acid solution when reacted with calcium carbonate.	

> ## Chapter 12
Preparation of salts

IN THIS CHAPTER YOU WILL:

Science skills:

- describe the nature of salts as the products of the neutralisation of acids

- understand and describe how soluble salts can be prepared by several different methods.

English skills:

- understand the use of prepositions in statements defining the relationship between events and consequences

- develop the use of the past passive, particularly in describing experimental methods.

Exercise 12.1 The nature of salts

IN THIS EXERCISE YOU WILL:

Science skills:

- look at the characteristic reactions of acids to produce salts.

English skills:

- learn how some verbs work with prepositions.

KEY WORDS

neutralisation: a chemical reaction between an acid and a base to produce a salt and water only; summarised by the ionic equation
$H^+(aq) + OH^-(aq) \rightarrow H_2O(l)$

salts: ionic compounds made by the neutralisation of an acid with a base (or alkali), e.g. copper(II) sulfate and potassium nitrate

LANGUAGE FOCUS

In English, some verbs work with a particular preposition, e.g. *listen to* and *look at*. This is important to remember, as it may be different in your language. In your language, do you need a preposition when you say these sentences?

Listen to the teacher.

Look at the thermometer.

You need to learn if a verb works with a preposition, and, if it does, which preposition. The easiest way to do this is to think of and memorise a key sentence for each verb.

Three verbs that are frequently used in chemistry, and that work with a preposition, are *depend*, *consist* and *result*. Look at these examples and notice the preposition:

The type of salt formed <u>depends on</u> *the acid used in preparing it.*

All salts <u>consist of</u> *ions.*

The neutralisation of an acid with an alkali <u>results in</u> *the formation of a salt.*

Note: any adjective or participle related to a verb usually works with the same preposition as the verb, e.g. *dependent on, consisting of*:

Salts are compounds <u>consisting of</u> *a positive metal or ammonium ion combined with a negative non-metal ion.*

The method of preparing a salt is <u>dependent on</u> *whether it is soluble or not.*

1   A base will neutralise an acid, and in the process a **salt** is formed.

    a   Circle the correct preposition in each of the following sentences.

        i   The pH of a solution depends **of / on** the hydrogen ion concentration of the solution.

        ii   A salt is an ionic compound consisting **in / of** a positive ion and a negative non-metal ion from an acid.

        iii   Litmus paper turns red or blue in a solution depending **on / of** whether the solution is acidic or alkaline.

    b   Complete the following statements about salts and their formation from acids choosing from these words:

        consist of   **consisting of**   **depends on**   **dependent on**

                depending on   **results in**

        i   All salts are ionic compounds. Most salts .... positive metal ions combined with negative non-metal ions.

        ii   The **neutralisation** of an acid with an alkali .... the formation of a salt and water as the only products.

iii   The type of salt formed .... the acid used in the neutralisation reaction.

iv   The metal present in the salt is .... the base, or alkali, used to react with the acid.

v   The method of preparing a salt .... whether the salt is soluble or insoluble in water.

c   Complete the following sentences using the prepositions given and your own words.

in   of   on

i   The acidity of a solution depends ....

....

ii   Adding an alkali to an acid results ....

....

iii   Salts are ionic compounds consisting ....

....

Exercise 12.2 The preparation of salts

IN THIS EXERCISE YOU WILL:

Science skills:

- describe a method for the preparation of salts.

English skills:

- use the passive voice in the past to write a report.

KEY WORD

filtrate: the liquid that passes through the filter paper during filtration

LANGUAGE FOCUS

In Chapter 6, you practised forming and using the passive form in the present. When you know how to form the passive in the present, it is easy to form the passive in the past. Here are the steps to remind you.

1 Think: what would the object of the active sentence be? That is the 'thing' that the verb is acting on. This becomes the subject of the new sentence.

2 Choose between *was* or *were (the past of be) and put it after your new subject.* Use *was* if the word in front of it is singular and *were* if it is plural.

3 Next, use the past participle of the verb. When you see three forms of a verb given – such as *take/took/taken* – the past participle is the third form. Put the participle after *was/were.*

4 Write the rest of the sentence.

Here is an example:

Past active: *We added the solid calcium carbonate to the acid using a spatula.*

Past passive: [1]*The solid calcium carbonate* [2]*was* [3]*added to the acid using a spatula.*

You often use the active when you speak, e.g. to your teacher. However, it is more scientific to use the passive when you write because the action is important, not the person who is doing the action.

2 Amina and Jacob carried out an experiment to prepare magnesium chloride. They used the reaction between magnesium carbonate and dilute hydrochloric acid.

magnesium carbonate + hydrochloric acid $\rightarrow$ magnesium chloride + water + carbon dioxide

They then used filtration and evaporation to separate magnesium chloride from the mixture.

This is Amina and Jacob's practical report:

We used a measuring cylinder to add $25\,cm^3$ of dilute hydrochloric acid to a beaker. Then we added some solid magnesium carbonate to the acid in the beaker. We stirred the reaction mixture with a glass rod. We carefully added more solid to the acid in small amounts so that the mixture didn't froth out of the beaker. We added further solid until there was no more fizzing and some solid was left in the bottom of the beaker. We stirred the mixture and filtered it to remove the excess solid. We then put the **filtrate** into an evaporating basin and heated it. We heated the filtrate until crystals formed at the edges of the solution. We removed the Bunsen burner and left the solution to cool slowly. After a time, we filtered off the crystals and dried them between pieces of filter paper.

LANGUAGE TIP

In spoken English, you often hear *didn't, can't, aren't, wasn't,* etc. However, science prefers the more formal, slightly longer *did not, cannot, are not, was not,* etc.

This is a good way to describe their experiment to a friend or to a teacher.
However, a better way to write the report as a scientist is using the passive.

a   Look at the first five sentences of Amina and Jacob's report. Rewrite them in
    the passive, using the Language Focus box to help you. The first one has been
    done for you.

    i   We used a measuring cylinder to add 25 cm³ of dilute hydrochloric acid
        to a beaker.

        A measuring cylinder was used to add 25 cm³ of dilute
        hydrochloric acid to a beaker.

    ii Then we added some solid magnesium carbonate to the acid in
        the beaker.

        Then some solid magnesium carbonate ....

        ....

    iii We stirred the reaction mixture with a glass rod.

        The reaction mixture ....

        ....

    iv We carefully added more solid to the acid in small amounts so that the
        mixture didn't froth out of the beaker.

        More solid ....

        ....

    v   We added further solid until there was no more fizzing and some solid
        was left in the bottom of the beaker.

        Further solid ....

        ....

b   Now rewrite the rest of Amina and Jacob's report on the experiment.
    Use the past passive.

    The mixture ....

    ....

    ....

    ....

    ....

    ....

    ....

Exercise 12.3 Reacting solutions: titration

IN THIS EXERCISE YOU WILL:

Science skills:

- investigate how the idea of the mole can be applied to solutions, especially in acid–base titrations used to prepare soluble salts.

English skills:

- practise how to express concentrations in spoken and written form.

KEY WORDS

acid–base titration: a method of quantitative chemical analysis where an acid is added slowly to a base until it has been neutralised

crystallisation: the process of forming crystals from a saturated solution

LANGUAGE FOCUS

In science, when you give quantities, you need to know both the written 'mathematical' language, and the spoken language. In Chapter 5, you saw how to express mathematical processes like *add*, *multiply*, and so on. You also need to be able to say things like $1\,mol/dm^3$, $0.5\,mol/dm^3$ or $10\,g/dm^3$.

For '/' say *per*. *per* means 'for each': *I have two chemistry lessons per week.*

For '³' say *cubic* or *cubed*. For example, $20\,cm^3$ = *twenty cubic centimetres* or *twenty centimetres cubed*.

For 'dm' say *decimetres*.

(You can also say the letters of the unit of volume; for example, *twenty cee em cubed or twenty dee em cubed.*)

For 'g' say *grams*.

So:

$1\,mol/dm^3$ is *one mole per cubic decimetre* or *one mole per decimetre cubed*; and $10\,g/dm^3$ means *10 grams per decimetre cubed*.

Remember that $1\,dm^3 = 1000\,cm^3\,(= 1$ litre).

So:

$1\,mol/dm^3$ is *one mole per cubic decimetre = one mole per one thousand cubic centimetres.*

CONTINUED

The mole is the measure of amount of substance and is very useful in helping to define the concentration of solutions. For example, for a concentration of $1\,mol/dm^3$, we say *one mole per decimetre cubed*. See Chapter 5 for more on the mole.

3 **a** Complete the following concentration values by writing the mathematical expression in words.

     i $0.1\,mol/dm^3 =$ ....

        ....

     ii $0.5\,mol/dm^3 =$ ....

        ....

     iii $20\,g/dm^3 =$ ....

        ....

     iv $0.2\,mol$ per $200\,cm^3 = 1\,mol/dm^3 =$ ....

        ....

  b We can write that the concentration of solution is $2\,mol/dm^3$. If we think about the units of concentration, this will help us to see how to calculate concentration.

     i What quantity is measured in moles? ....

     ii What quantity is measured in centimetres cubed or decimetres cubed?

        ....

     iii You can now practise how to say these concentrations. Work with a partner. One of you is A, one of you is B (see Figure 12.1). Choose three of the quantities in your bubble and say them aloud to your partner. Ask your partner to point to the correct quantity.

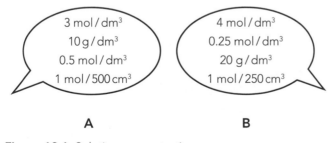

Figure 12.1: Solution concentrations.

4   **Acid–base titrations** can be used in analysis but can also be used to make soluble salts (see Figure 12.2).

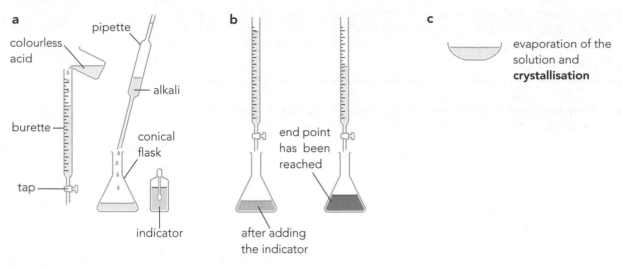

Figure 12.2: An acid–base titration to prepare a soluble salt.

Use information from Figure 12.2 and the words below to complete the following summary of **a–c**.

acid   burette   colour   crystallised   end point

evaporated   filtered   indicator   pipette   volume

a   The .... is filled with ...., and a known .... of alkali is added to the conical flask using a volumetric ....

b   The acid is added to the alkali until the .... just changes ....; this is the .... for the titration.

c   The solution is .... and crystallised. Finally, the crystals are .... and carefully dried.

› Chapter 13
The Periodic Table

IN THIS CHAPTER YOU WILL:

Science skills:

- describe the structure of the Periodic Table into groups and periods based on the elements being organised by increasing atomic number

- understand that the properties of the elements vary in a repeating (periodic) way.

English skills:

- develop the vocabulary involved in describing the organisation of the Periodic Table

- practise using the definite/indefinite articles and pronouns in constructing sentences.

Exercise 13.1 Introducing the Periodic Table

IN THIS EXERCISE YOU WILL:

Science skills:

- consider how elements in different regions of the Periodic Table show similar characteristic properties.

English skills:

- become familiar with the terms for different sections of the Periodic Table.

KEY WORDS

Periodic Table: a table of elements arranged in order of increasing proton number (atomic number) to show the similarities of the chemical elements with related electron configurations

1   The main distinction in the **Periodic Table** is between metals and non-metals. The non-metals are grouped into the top right-hand region of the Periodic Table, above the thick, stepped line in Figure 13.1.

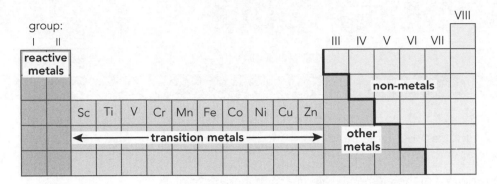

Figure 13.1: Distribution of metals and non-metals in the Periodic Table.

The elements are organised in vertical groups, which have similar chemical and physical properties. Some of these groups have both names and numbers. Between Groups II and III of the table, there is a block of metals known as the transition elements (or transition metals).

Find and circle 11 words in the wordsearch puzzle, then use the words to complete clues **a–h** about key features of the Periodic Table. The words may be arranged horizontally, vertically or diagonally.

T	O	I	O	H	E	G	R	O	U	P	S	O	C
L	A	N	O	I	T	I	S	N	A	R	T	A	T
N	E	E	L	A	T	N	O	Z	I	R	O	H	G
O	I	G	H	N	O	L	S	N	E	R	H	A	N
B	A	O	E	A	Z	E	D	N	N	R	R	L	E
L	L	R	O	A	O	S	O	O	H	O	L	O	O
E	K	D	I	T	T	T	I	N	H	E	L	G	O
I	A	Y	T	E	S	N	R	M	S	N	E	E	N
I	L	H	R	H	E	S	E	E	R	L	N	T
L	I	L	T	O	S	N	P	T	L	O	E	E	A
I	N	E	R	R	A	O	M	A	P	I	U	R	T
L	E	N	E	O	G	E	E	L	N	P	I	S	I
R	V	E	R	T	I	C	A	L	E	D	N	L	M
E	P	R	L	N	G	S	T	N	E	M	E	L	E

LANGUAGE TIP

English is used internationally and some speakers spell words slightly differently, although the meaning is the same. For example, 'British spelling' = *aluminium / organise / colour / analyse / modelling*; 'American spelling' = *aluminum / organize / color / analyze / modeling*.

a   the first element in the table: ....

b   the general name for an element in Group VII: ....

c   an element in the right-hand region of the table: ....

d   the name for the .... columns of the table: ....

e   the name for the unreactive gases on the right: ....

f   the name for a .... row in the table: ....

g   the block of elements in the centre: .... metals

h   the table contains only: ....

Exercise 13.2 The organisation of the Periodic Table

IN THIS EXERCISE YOU WILL:

Science skills:

*   recognise that the chemical elements show a periodic variation in properties when organised by increasing atomic number.

English skills:

*   develop the language to describe periodic change, and the use of the definite article.

2   a   Read the following passage about the origins and basis of the modern Periodic Table. Then put a tick (✓) in the correct column in the table to indicate whether the statements are True or False.

When the first attempts to construct the Periodic Table were made, nobody knew about the structure of the atom. The order of the elements originally followed their increasing atomic masses, which could be measured experimentally. However, it was later found that proton (atomic) number is a better basis for ordering the elements. Atomic number provides a linear, continuous sequence for listing the elements. However, the Periodic Table is a two-dimensional representation, which is obtained by splitting the continuous list into sections. These sections are then placed below each other, to form something resembling a wall. The sequence of elements is split according to the structure of the energy levels (shells) of electrons in the atom.

There is now a direct link between the properties of an element, its position in the table and its electronic configuration (see Figure 13.2). Elements in the same group of the table have the same number of electrons in their outer shell. We also know that, as you move across a period in the table, a shell of electrons is being filled. Each period in the table represents the filling of an energy level.

Groups

	I	II		III	IV	V	VI	VII	VIII
1								1 H	2 He
2	2,1 Li	2,2 Be		2,3 B	2,4 C	2,5 N	2,6 O	2,7 F	2,8 Ne
3	2,8,1 Na	2,8,2 Mg		2,8,3 Al	2,8,4 Si	2,8,5 P	2,8,6 S	2,8,7 Cl	2,8,8 Ar
4	2,8,8,1 K	2,8,8,2 Ca							

Periods

Figure 13.2: Relationship between an element's position in the Periodic Table and its electronic configuration.

Statement	True	False
The first attempts to make a table of the elements placed them in order of increasing atomic mass.		
The sequence of the elements is the same, whether it is based on their proton number or their atomic mass.		
The sequence of the elements is split into rows, based on the electron shells being filled in their atoms.		
The splitting of the sequence of elements gives us a table consisting of horizontal groups and vertical periods.		
Usually, as you move down a group in the Periodic Table, the number of electrons in the outer shell of the atoms is the same.		
The first row of the table only has two elements in it, because the first electron shell can only hold two electrons.		
All the elements in Group VII of the table have eight electrons in their outer shell.		

b   Find words with the meanings given in the passage in part **a**. Write the words on the lines provided.

i   does not stop; uninterrupted (adjective): ....

ii   arranged in two directions (adjective): ....

    iii   organisation of the electrons in an atom (adjective + noun):

        ....

    iv   vertical column of elements (noun): ....

    v   horizontal row of elements (noun): ....

    vi   at the edge of an atom (adjective + noun): ....

    vii   orbit in which electrons are found (adjective + noun): ....

3   One physical property that shows a periodic change is [1]the melting point of an element. Figure 13.3 is a bar chart of [2]the melting points of [3]the elements in Periods 2 and 3, plotted against [4]the proton number of each element. [5]The chart shows how [6]the melting points vary in a repeated pattern. [7]The melting points of the elements in Groups III and IV show [8]the highest values in each period.

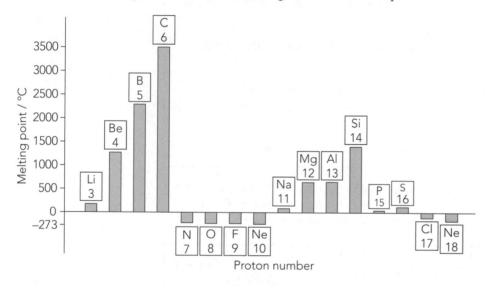

Figure 13.3: Periodic variation in the melting points of the elements in Periods 2 and 3 of the Periodic Table.

LANGUAGE FOCUS

The word *the* is called the definite article. There is only one form:

the scientist, the scientists, the test-tube

It has several different uses; let's look at three:

A   When there is only one of something, or when everyone knows which one we are talking about:

    Look at <u>the</u> moon! (Our planet only has one moon.)

    Look at <u>the</u> board. (There are many boards in the world, but only one in this room.)

CONTINUED

Can you light the Bunsen burner, please? (There are several in the lab, but only one in front of us – 'our' Bunsen burner.)

B When something has been mentioned before and we now know what is being talked about. The first mention is often *a* or *an*, but after that *the* is used:

Take a test-tube from the rack. Add some zinc powder to the test-tube and then 5 cm³ of dilute hydrochloric acid.

We carried out an experiment. The aim of the experiment was to react sodium safely with water.

C At the start of a phrase with *of* or *in* + noun:

The study of metal reactivity with acids shows that copper is less reactive than zinc.

The elements in the Periodic Table are arranged in order of the proton number of the atoms.

Note: *the* is not used when making a generalisation, e.g. about all metals. *The* refers to something specific, so it is not appropriate in generalisations:

Metals are generally good conductors of electricity and heat.

a There are eight examples of *the* underlined in the paragraph at the start of question **2**. Find them in the passage, then match them to uses **A–C** in the Language Focus box by writing **A**, **B** or **C** in the following grid.

1	the melting point	
2	the melting points	
3	the elements	
4	the proton number	

5	The chart	
6	the melting points	
7	The melting points	
8	the highest values	

b Circle the correct options to complete the following paragraph on the nature of the Periodic Table. If no word is required, simply circle the dash (**–**).

Why is **a / the** table of elements called the Periodic Table? The name comes from the fact that when the elements are arranged in sequence, we see **the / a** repeated pattern in the properties of the elements. The repeated patterns are seen in both physical and chemical properties. **The / –** atomic numbers are important when organising the elements. **The / an** arrangement of **– / the** elements in the table is based on their increasing atomic number. There is **the / a** direct connection between **the / –** organisation of the elements into groups and periods (rows) and their electronic configuration.

Exercise 13.3 Trends in the Periodic Table

N THIS EXERCISE YOU WILL:

Science skills:

- describe how the properties of the elements vary across the Periodic Table and in different groups.

English skills:

- use pronouns correctly in your discussion of ideas.

KEY WORDS

halogens: elements in Group VII of the Periodic Table – generally the most reactive group of non-metals

noble gases: elements in Group VIII – a group of stable, very unreactive gases

LANGUAGE FOCUS

In scientific texts, you often find the pronouns *they*, *it*, *them*, *their* and *its*, and you need to be able to understand what these words are referring to. Writers often use them, because it means that they do not have to repeat the nouns in a text again and again. When you see *it*, *its*, *they*, *their* or *them*, try to find and circle the information they refer to.

For example:

Aluminium is the most common metal in Earth's crust. However, [1]it is too reactive to occur naturally as a free metal. [2]Its major ore is bauxite, which contains aluminium oxide. In 1886, Hall and Heroult made an important breakthrough. [3]They developed a method of electrolysis to produce pure aluminium from the oxide. [4]Their method meant that aluminium could be produced economically in large amounts. There are many very important uses of aluminium; aircraft construction is one example of [5]them.

The singular pronouns *it / its* in the passage mean (aluminium). However, the plural pronouns *they*, *their* and *them* refer to different things: the scientists and the uses. How do you know? Usually, you look in front (left) of the pronoun for the nearest plural noun; if it makes logical sense, it is the word being referenced. Look in front of [3] and [4], and you find (Hall and Heroult). Look in front of [5], and you find (very important uses).

Remember not to use a pronoun the first time you mention something in science.

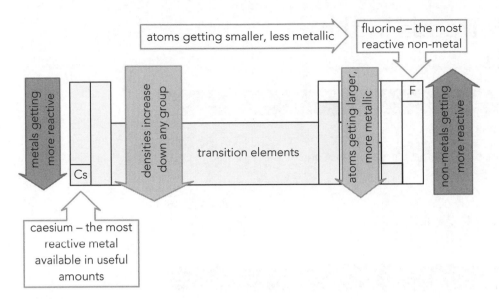

Figure 13.4: General trends in the Periodic Table, apart from the **noble gases** in Group VIII.

4   The following statements relate to information given in Figure 13.4. Rewrite the statements, replacing the words underlined with *it*, *its*, *they*, *them* or *their*.

   a   Sodium is a highly reactive metal in Group I. <u>Sodium</u> reacts vigorously with cold water.

   ....

   ....

   b   Transition elements form a block in the middle of the Periodic Table. <u>Transition elements</u> are especially useful, strong metals.

   ....

   ....

   ....

   c   Fluorine is the most reactive of the elements in Group VII. <u>Fluorine</u> can react explosively, and <u>fluorine</u> will displace other **halogens** from compounds.

   ....

   ....

   ....

   d   Atoms of the elements get smaller as we move across a period in the table. As <u>the atoms</u> get smaller, the elements concerned become less metallic.

   ....

   ....

   ....

e   The elements of Group I are very reactive, and <u>the elements'</u> reactivity increases as we go down the group.

....

....

....

5   Read the passage, then complete the grid with the information referred to by pronouns **1–7**. The first one has been done for you.

Most of the elements can be classified as metals. ¹They are positioned to the left in the Periodic Table. Metals are held together by metallic bonding. This type of bonding gives rise to many metallic properties. However, there is wide variation in the level of ²their properties when looked at in detail. For instance, many metals have high density (e.g. iron), but the alkali metals do not. ³They have low densities and float on water.

Non-metals lie to the right of the table. ⁴Their properties tend to be the opposite of metals'. There is a transition from metals to non-metals as we move from left to right in the table; ⁵it is one of the main trends present in the table. The best way to identify a metal or non-metal is to check whether ⁶it conducts electricity or not. Electrical conductivity is a key property of a metal such as copper, and is a major reason for ⁷its use in cabling and domestic wiring.

> **LANGUAGE TIP**
>
> *Tend to* is a useful verb in both scientific and general English. Use it before a verb to mean 'usually':
>
> *Metals and non-metals <u>tend to have</u> opposite properties.*
>
> *She <u>tends to go</u> for a swim at weekends.*

Pronoun number	What the pronoun is referring to
1	metals
2	
3	
4	
5	
6	
7	

> Chapter 14

Metallic elements and alloys

> [!NOTE] IN THIS CHAPTER YOU WILL:
>
> **Science skills:**
>
> - describe the characteristic properties of metals and some methods of testing their salts
>
> - understand the importance of alloys and their design and use for specific purposes.
>
> **English skills:**
>
> - develop the language used to describe metals and alloys
>
> - describe the tests used in identifying metal salts and express the test results.

Exercise 14.1 The properties of metals

> [!NOTE] IN THIS EXERCISE YOU WILL:
>
> **Science skills:**
>
> - look at the general properties of metals and relate them to the type of bonding present.
>
> **English skills:**
>
> - develop your vocabulary and practice using key terms to describe the properties and type of bonding in metals.

1 a Metals have certain common properties that differ from those of non-metals. Fill in the rows of the word puzzle about the properties of metals. Use the clues given.

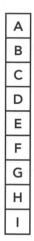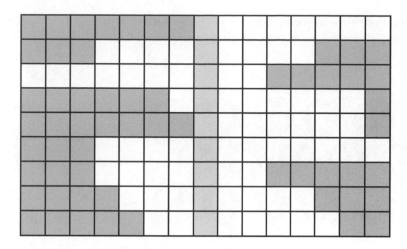

A   Potassium is more … than sodium.

B   This property means that metals can be beaten or hammered into sheets. Metals are ….

C   These parts of an electrolysis cell are made of a metal or graphite.

D   This is the metal below potassium in Group I of the Periodic Table.

E   Metals … heat and electricity.

F   This is the method used to extract aluminium from bauxite and purify (refine) copper.

G   Metals can be stretched into wire. Metals are ….

H   Carbon … is the gas that reduces iron oxide to iron in the blast furnace.

I   Metals ring like a bell when hit with a hammer. Metals are ….

b   The highlighted word in the word puzzle is one of the types of reaction that we saw in Chapter 10. Give two different definitions for this chemical process:

1   ……………………… is the …………………………………………………

……………………………………………………………………………

2   ……………………… is the …………………………………………………

……………………………………………………………………………

c   Several of these properties of metals occur because of the distinctive type of chemical bonding in metals known as **metallic bonding** (see Figure 14.1).

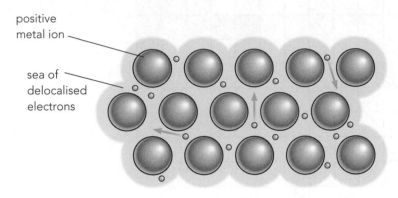

positive metal ion

sea of delocalised electrons

Figure 14.1: Metallic bonding.

Complete the passage using the words below. Not all of the words are needed.

between	conduct	ductile	heat	lattice

lose	metallic	regular	positive	string

stronger   under

In a metal the atoms are arranged in an organised, ... structure called a .... The metal atoms .... their outer electrons into a 'sea of delocalised electrons'. The more electrons each atom loses, the .... the bonding. The presence of this 'sea of delocalised electrons' which can move .... the .... metal ions is the reason metals .... electricity and .... well. The layers of ions can also move over each other without breaking the .... bonding. This is why metals are both malleable and ....

Exercise 14.2 Analysis of metal salts

IN THIS EXERCISE YOU WILL:

Science skills:

- look at the analytical tests for metal salts.

English skills:

- use key words and learn how to describe analytical tests for metal salts.

2 A set of experimental tests can help us identify an unknown salt by telling us which metal and non-metal ions are present. Using the following table, match the meanings (**A–E**) to the key words (**1–5**) and enter the letter in the answer grid. One example has been done for you.

Key word	Example of use		Meaning
1 excess	an <u>excess</u> of sodium hydroxide is added	A	the precipitate formed goes back into solution
2 re-dissolves	the solid that had just formed <u>redissolves</u> when more ammonia is added	B	a solution of a substance in a small amount of water
3 splint	the glowing <u>splint</u> relit, showing oxygen was present	C	more than enough
4 bleaches	chlorine <u>bleaches</u> wet litmus paper	D	the colour is turned white
5 concentrated	<u>concentrated</u> sodium hydroxide is added	E	a thin strip of wood

1	2	3	4	5
				B

3 Mayur wrote the following description of the test for a carbonate. He used more key words that are useful in writing about the test. Read his description, then find the words to match the meanings and write them in the table.

> We can test to see whether a solid is a carbonate by reacting it with dilute hydrochloric acid. When the acid is added, the solid dissolves and fizzing takes place. The gas given off is carbon dioxide. If we bubble the gas through a clear, colourless solution of limewater, a white precipitate is formed. The solution turns milky.

Key word	Meaning
....	a solution of a substance in a large amount of water (noun)
....	bubbles of gas forming (noun / -ing form)
....	the solid disappears, forming a solution (verb)
....	a solid suddenly formed by mixing two solutions or passing a gas into a solution (noun)
....	transparent and can be seen through (adjective)
....	has no colour (adjective)
....	cloudy white in colour (adjective)

LANGUAGE TIP

Remember that prefixes help you understand words. When you see words that start with *re-*, e.g. *redissolve*, *relight* or *resend*, it means 'again': *dissolve again, light again, send again.*

LANGUAGE FOCUS

When you describe a test in chemistry, remember these simple tips:

1   Write in the present simple. The present simple is the form of the verb with s at the end of *he/she/it* verbs in the affirmative:

The solution turns clear/cloudy/milky.

It reacts vigorously.

Also remember that, when the subject is plural, the verb has no s at the end:

They react vigorously.

2   Use the present passive when appropriate. This is the form with *am/are/is* + *-ed*/past participle.

The gas is passed through the limewater to test it.

Crystals are formed at the bottom of the dish.

3   Use *When* + present, present to give information about when, for example, changes occur:

When the acid is added, the solid reacts strongly.

4   Use *If* + present, present to give, for example, recommendations:

If we use a pipette, we can measure out an accurate volume.

5   Use useful phrases to help you build your sentences. For example:

… to see whether… (+ subject + verb = aim of the test or step in test)

by… (+ *-ing* = for a process or action taken)

    aim of test   process
We can test to see whether the gas is oxygen by holding a glowing splint in it.

6   Use key words, e.g. *dissolve, fizzing, to bubble, reacting.*

When you read Mayur's description again, can you find examples of all these things?

4   Figure 14.2 shows how tests were performed on a white solid to prove it was a zinc sulfate.

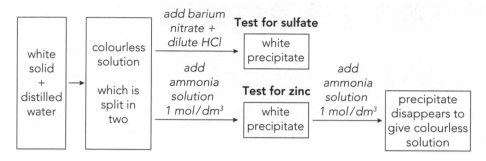

Figure 14.2: Flow diagram for testing a white solid.

Write a description of what is happening in each of the two tests in Figure 14.2. Use the key words from questions **1** and **2** and the Language Focus box to help you.

a   Test for sulfate:

We can test to see whether the salt is a sulfate using acidified barium nitrate solution. The white powder was dissolved in distilled water. This gave ....

....

....

....

....

....

....

b   Test for zinc:

....

....

....

....

....

....

....

....

Exercise 14.3 Alloys

IN THIS EXERCISE YOU WILL:

Science skills:

- look at the important features and usefulness of alloys.

English skills:

- use the preposition *for* when describing the principal use or purpose of something.

KEY WORD

alloys: mixtures of elements (usually metals) designed to have the properties useful for a particular purpose; e.g. solder (an alloy of tin and lead) has a low melting point

Whereas some iron produced in a blast furnace is used directly, most is converted to steel. Steel is probably the most important **alloy** we make.

5   a   Complete the following paragraphs by circling the correct word for each gap **1–14** from the numbered choices in the table.

An **alloy** is generally a mixture of two or more metals. For instance, **1** … is a mixture of **2** … and zinc. All types of steel contain the non-metal, **3** …. Some types of steel also contain **4** … metals. Whereas iron itself rusts easily, **5** … steel is resistant to rusting because of the presence of **6** ….

Alloys are formed in the **7** …, or liquid, state. This means that the different metals can be well mixed together. When cooled, the metallic alloy is formed as a crystal **8** … held together by **9** … bonding. The alloys keep the typical properties of a metal. They conduct heat and **10** … well. They are also malleable and **11** ….

The structure of an alloy is similar to a pure metal. The **12** … metal ions are arranged in layers. There is a 'sea of **13** …. electrons' bonding the layers together. However, the other metal ions present can change the properties. For example, ions with a different size can make it more difficult for the layers to **14** … over each other.

Gap		Gap	
1	gold / brass / silver	8	lattice / net / string
2	tin / chromium / copper	9	ionic / covalent / metallic
3	sulfur / carbon / boron	10	sound / electricity / waves
4	transition / alkali / noble	11	ductile / elastic / fragile
5	tungsten / mild / stainless	12	negative / neutral / positive
6	chromium / tin / aluminium	13	fixed / delocalised / localised
7	solid / molten / elastic	14	slide / stick /crunch

LANGUAGE TIP

As you have seen, using linkers (connectives) to connect ideas improves scientific writing style – and the greater the variety of linkers you use, the better your style. For example, use *whereas* in place of *but* to connect two contrasting ideas.

LANGUAGE FOCUS

When you want to describe the principal use for something, use *for*.
For is a preposition, so it can only have a noun (e.g. *lunch, chemistry, school*),
a pronoun (e.g. *me, them, that*) or an *-ing* form of a verb (e.g. *building,
recording, heating*). This means that if you want to express a verb or an action,
you will need to use the *-ing* form:

Aluminium is used for mak<u>ing</u> airplanes.

Copper is used for wir<u>ing</u> in electrical circuits.

A thermometer is used for measur<u>ing</u> temperature.

b   Use the information in Table 14.1 about alloys to complete the sentences in
parts **i–iv**.

Alloy	Typical composition		Properties	Uses
mild steel	iron	99.7%	stronger and harder than pure iron but can be shaped	car bodies and to construct large structures
	carbon	0.3%		
stainless steel	iron	79.9%	harder than pure iron, does not rust	to manufacture cutlery, surgical equipment and reaction vessels in chemical industry
	chromium	18%		
	nickel	10%		
	carbon	0.1%		
brass	copper	70%	harder than pure copper, 'gold' coloured	decorative fittings in buildings
	zinc	30%		
solder	tin	50%	lower melting point	to join metals in electronics
	lead	50%		

Table 14.1: Some important alloys.

i   **Mild steel** is used for .... because it is ....

....

ii   **Solder** is used for .... because it has ....

....

iii   **Stainless steel** is used for .... because it is ....

....

iv   **Brass** is used for .... because it is ....

....

Chapter 15

Reactivity of metals

IN THIS CHAPTER YOU WILL:

Science skills:

- investigate the differences in reactivity of metals from different parts of the Periodic Table

- understand how metal displacement reactions can help construct a reactivity series of metals.

English skills:

- use adverbs to describe actions, and develop your ability to comment on interrelated changes happening at the same time

- use useful expressions to write hypotheses, predictions and conclusions.

Exercise 15.1 Comparing metal reactivity

IN THIS EXERCISE YOU WILL:

Science skills:

- look at the differences in the reactivity of metals from different regions of the Periodic Table.

English skills:

- learn to use adverbs to describe how things happen.

1   The properties of the transition metals contrast with those of the alkali metals. Use this idea to complete the table.

Property	Alkali metals	Transition metals
hardness	soft	....
melting point	low	....
density	....	high density
colour of solid salts	....	often coloured
reactivity	....	moderately reactive

> **LANGUAGE TIP**
>
> The word *contrast* can be a verb (conTRAST) or a noun (CONtrast). As a verb, use it with *with*; as a noun, it usually goes before *to* or in the phrase *in contrast to*.

2   The differences in reactivity of the metals can be shown by their reactions with water and air.

LANGUAGE FOCUS

Adverbs do a similar job to adjectives: they describe. However, adjectives describe things and people (nouns), whereas adverbs describe actions (verbs). Most 'how' adverbs are easy to form: simply add -ly to an adjective:

slow – slowly: quick – quickly,

The process is slow. (process = noun)

It melted slowly. (melted = verb)

The colourless solution evaporated quickly. (colourless + noun)
(verb + quickly)

Adverbs of manner can give you information about actions and they answer the question *How?*:

How does it evaporate? *It evaporates quickly.*

How does magnesium burn? *It burns very brightly.*

Can you see where adverbs of manner go in a sentence? After the verb and as near it as possible.

a   Complete the table using the adverbs of manner given. Then complete the balanced equation for the reaction between potassium and water in the bottom row.

slowly   steadily   strongly   violently

Element	Reaction with water	Reaction with air	
lithium	reacts .... $2Li + 2H_2O \rightarrow$ $2LiOH + H_2$	tarnishes .... to give a layer of oxide	
sodium	reacts .... $2Na + 2H_2O \rightarrow$ $2NaOH + H_2$	tarnishes quickly to give a layer of oxide	increasing reactivity ↓
potassium	reacts .... $2K + 2H_2O \rightarrow$	tarnishes very quickly to give a layer of oxide	

b   Complete the sentences with the adverb form of the correct adjective.

Example: Sodium reacts <u>strongly</u> with cold water. (**strong** / ~~poor~~)

   i   Magnesium burns .... in air with a white flame.
       (**poor / brilliant**)

   ii   Caesium is a metal low down in Group I and it reacts

        .... with water. (**explosive / slow**)

   iii The reaction between magnesium and cold water takes place very

        .... (**quick / slow**)

   iv Copper is a chemically unreactive metal and conducts heat

        .... (**strong / poor**)

Exercise 15.2 Trends in reactivity in the Periodic Table

IN THIS EXERCISE YOU WILL:

Science skills:

- describe trends in reactivity in the Periodic Table.

English skills:

- use comparative forms to talk about interrelated changes that happen at the same time.

LANGUAGE FOCUS

As you saw in Chapters 8 and 11, the comparative of an adjective is formed with -er, more/less... (+ than):

A 0.2 mol/dm³ solution of sodium hydroxide is <u>less</u> concentrated <u>than</u> a 0.5 mol/dm³ solution.

Comparatives can also be used to express change:

When a metal rod gets hot<u>ter</u>, it expands. = comparative expresses change in temperature

As the metal gets <u>less</u> flexible, it may break. = comparative expresses change in flexibility

Sometimes, however, you want to express two changes that occur at the same time, and that are directly related to each other. For example:

When you increase the temperature of a liquid, the atoms start to move faster.

You can express this more neatly by saying:

The hotter the liquid becomes, the faster the atoms move.

So *the* + comparative..., *the* + comparative...

CONTINUED

Notice: the comparative here can be a comparative adjective (*hotter, more nervous*) or *less / more* + subject + verb:

The <u>more</u> a metal rod is heated, the <u>more</u> it expands.

The <u>more</u> nervous she is about a test, the <u>less</u> she remembers.

3   a   i   Write the comparative forms of the adjectives. Remember that one is irregular (see Chapter 8).

far   great   low

....

reactive

.... / less ....

ii   Use the five comparatives from part **i** to complete this paragraph.

There are certain patterns of reactivity that apply to the position of an element in the Periodic Table:

The lower a metal is within a group, the .... that metal is: reactivity becomes .... as you go down a group of metals.

The .... a metal is across a period, the less reactive that metal is; in Period 3 the reactivity decreases in the order, sodium > magnesium > aluminium.

In Group VII (the halogens), the .... the element in the group, the less reactive it is; reactivity becomes .... as you go down a group of non-metals.

b   Tick the correct box to indicate what the completed paragraph in part **a ii** is about:

i   How the reactivity of an element always decreases down a group in the Periodic Table.   ☐

ii   How the reactivity of an element increases across a period in the Periodic Table.   ☐

iii   How the reactivity of the elements varies depending on their position in the Periodic Table.   ☐

Exercise 15.3 Experiments on the reactivity of metals

IN THIS EXERCISE YOU WILL:

Science skills:

- look at designing experiments to compare the reactivities of metals.

English skills:

- learn how to state a hypothesis and write predictions for an experiment.

KEY WORD

reactivity: the ease with which a chemical substance takes part in a chemical reaction

LANGUAGE FOCUS

Planning investigations is an important aspect of practical work. Stating the hypothesis behind an experiment and making predictions are key skills in setting up the experiment.

In Chapter 9, you saw how to use *will*, *could*, *may*, *might* and *should* to make hypotheses/predictions. Sometimes, however, you want to express a hypothesis or prediction using *if* to give a particular condition. To do this, use the structure called the first conditional.

If one metal is more reactive than another, it will displace the less reactive one from solution.

       This is the condition.   This is the prediction.

<u>*If an alkali is added to an acid in the correct amount,*</u> *it should produce a neutral solution.*

<u>*If $Ba(NO_3)_2$ solution is added to*</u> *NaCl solution, it will produce a white precipitate.*

4   Complete the following sentence halves with the correct form of the verb in brackets.

    a   If a piece of sodium .... (*place*) on the surface of water,

    b   If moist red litmus paper .... (*hold*) in ammonia gas,

    c   If carbon dioxide gas .... (*bubble*) into limewater,

    d   If chlorine gas .... (*pass*) into potassium iodide solution,

Now match the sentence halves and write completed halves **a–d** on the correct lines **i–iv**.

    i   ...., it will turn cloudy.

    ii   ...., it will fizz and melt into a ball.

iii ...., it will turn brown.

iv ...., it will turn blue.

5 Chang and Jane are planning an experiment to see whether zinc is more reactive than silver by adding pieces of zinc metal to silver nitrate solution. Complete their hypotheses/predictions using the words below.

less   more   should   will

a If one metal is .... reactive than another, it .... displace the .... reactive metal from a solution.

b If zinc is more reactive than silver, it .... react when added to silver nitrate solution and we should see silver metal formed.

c If we add silver to zinc nitrate solution, we .... not see a reaction.

6 You are designing an experiment to put iron, copper and magnesium in order of their **reactivity**. You have strips of each metal and solutions of iron(II) sulfate, copper(II) sulfate and magnesium sulfate.

Write a hypothesis and some predictions for the experiment. Begin your hypothesis with phrases and connecting phrases such as:

If we use ...   If we test ...   If we carry out ...

We think that ...   By seeing which + verb ...   We expect to see...

Hypothesis

....

....

....

....

....

Predictions

....

....

....

....

....

Exercise 15.4 Interpreting displacement reactions

IN THIS EXERCISE YOU WILL:

Science skills:

- interpret the results of the displacement reactions proposed in Exercise 15.3 and draw conclusions.

English skills:

- become familiar with useful expressions to help you write your conclusions.

LANGUAGE FOCUS

An important skill in practical work is being able to draw conclusions from results. There are some useful expressions which can help you write about your conclusions:

To start a sentence: *This means that…, This suggests that…, We can conclude that…*

After a comma in the middle of a sentence: *…, suggesting that…, which means that…*

This means / suggests that magnesium is more reactive than zinc.

We can conclude that the reactivity of the alkali metals increases as we go down the group.

Magnesium displaces zinc from the solution, suggesting that magnesium is more reactive than zinc.

Potassium is below lithium in Group I, which means that it reacts more strongly with water.

7 a   Table 15.1 shows some observations from the experiment in question **3** of Exercise 15.3.

	Iron	Copper	Magnesium
iron(II) sulfate		no reaction	reaction – metal deposited; green colour of solution fades
copper(II) sulfate	reaction – metal deposited; blue colour of solution fades		reaction – metal deposited; blue colour of solution fades
magnesium sulfate	no reaction	no reaction	

Table 15.1: Experimental observations.

Complete these sentences to give the conclusion drawn from the practical observations.

i   When magnesium is placed in copper(II) sulfate solution, the blue colour of the solution fades, suggesting that ....

ii   There is no observed reaction when copper is placed in magnesium sulfate solution, which means that ....

....

iii There is a reaction when magnesium is placed in iron(II) sulfate solution. This means that ....

b i   Write the three metals in Table 15.1 in order of increasing reactivity.

.... < .... < ....

ii   Explain why you put the metals in this order. You should comment on all three metals and their reactions, if there are any. Some of the sentences have been started for you.

Iron reacted with .... solution, but it ....

.... This means that iron is ....

....

Copper did not react with ....

This suggests that ....

Magnesium reacts with ....

This means that ....

Therefore, we can conclude that .... is the most

.... of these metals, and .... is the least

.... of the three.

LANGUAGE TIP

The verb most frequently used with *conclusion* is *draw*; you *draw conclusions*. This is not related to art or pencils; it is from an old meaning of *draw*: 'to extract or pull' (e.g. *draw* teeth, *draw* curtains, *draw* a cart).

〉 Chapter 16

Extraction and corrosion of metals

IN THIS CHAPTER YOU WILL:

Science skills:

- describe the extraction of iron and aluminium from their ores by reduction

- understand how metals corrode on exposure to the atmosphere and discuss how different metals can be protected from this corrosion.

English skills:

- develop the vocabulary related to the extraction of metals and to protecting them from corrosion

- construct sentences describing the purpose of actions.

Exercise 16.1 The blast furnace

IN THIS EXERCISE YOU WILL:

Science skills:

- investigate the industrial extraction of iron.

English skills:

- practise the use of important terms for describing the extraction of iron in the blast furnace.

KEY WORDS

blast furnace: a furnace for extracting metals (particularly iron) by reduction with carbon that uses hot air blasted in at the base of the furnace to raise the temperature

hematite: the major ore of iron, iron(III) oxide

ore: a naturally occurring mineral from which a metal can be extracted

slag: a molten mixture of impurities, mainly calcium silicate, formed in the blast furnace

1   Iron is extracted from iron **ore** (**hematite**) by reduction. This major industrial
     process is carried out in a **blast furnace** (see Figure 16.1).

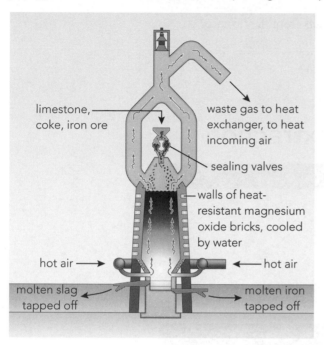

Figure 16.1: The blast furnace for the extraction of iron from iron ore.

a   The labels on Figure 16.1 contain some important terms. Match the terms
     1–8 with their definitions **A–H** in the answer grid. One example has been
     done for you.

Key words			Definition
1	limestone	A	a form of coal with a high carbon content
2	iron ore	B	liquid iron
3	waste gas	C	a sedimentary rock composed mostly of calcium carbonate – decomposes to give carbon dioxide in the furnace
4	**slag**	D	bricks of magnesium oxide that cover the inside of the furnace to keep the heat in and do not break up
5	heat-resistant bricks	E	hot gases, mainly nitrogen and carbon dioxide; recycled to heat the air blasted in at the bottom of the furnace
6	coke	F	a mineral containing iron dug from the ground; hematite (Fe_2O_3) is the main ore of iron
7	tapped off	G	waste material from the furnace that floats on the molten iron; used in road building
8	molten iron	H	run off – the liquid iron is run off at the bottom of the furnace

Key word	Definition
1	
2	F
3	
4	
5	
6	
7	
8	

b **i**   Which of the terms in the grid refer to materials mined from the ground?

....

ii   Which of the terms in the grid refer to products from the furnace?

....

iii   Which term listed in the grid is the odd one out?

....

Exercise 16.2 Aluminium extraction

IN THIS EXERCISE YOU WILL:

Science skills:

- investigate the industrial extraction of aluminium.

English skills:

- practise working out the meanings of words from context.

KEY WORDS

bauxite: the major ore of aluminium; a form of aluminium oxide, Al_2O_3

cryolite: sodium aluminium fluoride (Na_3AlF_6), an ore of aluminium used in the extraction of aluminium to lower the operating temperature of the electrolytic cell. Now replaced by synthetic sodium aluminium fluoride produced from the common mineral fluorite

LANGUAGE FOCUS

When you meet a new word in chemistry, you can often guess the meaning from context. This means looking at other information on the page to help you. For example, you used Figure 16.1 to help you match the words and definitions. You could understand some words, such as *sealing valve*, simply by looking at the diagram. If you see new words on diagrams, write your own sentence with the word in a notebook. This will help you remember it.

You can also work out the meanings of some new words when you read a text. Cover the new word with a finger and look at what the words around it tell you. You can often then guess the meaning. For example:

After mining, the iron is extracted from the [ore]. This is often done by [smelting].

Cover the word *ore*.

After mining, the iron is extracted from the ….

The words *mining*, *iron* and *extracted* tell you that the 'mystery' word refers to what iron is found in when it is mined. That gives you the basic meaning of *ore*: the rock that iron is found in. You can then see that *smelting* refers to a process used to extract iron from rock.

As you read a text, you find more and more clues.

You will remember words better if you make the effort to understand them from their context than if you use a dictionary, but remember to write them in your own example sentences.

---

2 a Read the passage, then fill in the different rows of the word puzzle using the clues given.

Aluminium is too reactive to be extracted by reduction of its ore by carbon. It must be obtained by electrolysis of aluminium oxide, sometimes known as alumina. **Bauxite** is the main mineral ore of aluminium. Aluminium oxide is purified from bauxite and is then used for electrolysis. **Cryolite** is another mineral containing aluminium. It is added to the molten aluminium oxide to lower the melting point of aluminium oxide. The aluminium oxide must be molten so that the ions can move to conduct the current. Aluminium ions move to the negative electrode where reduction takes place. The other product of this electrolysis is oxygen. The electrodes are made of graphite. At the high temperature of the electrolysis, the anode can react with the oxygen producing carbon dioxide gas.

LANGUAGE TIP

Must is stronger than *should*, and better scientific style than *have to*. Use it to say when something is necessary – either because it is the only way, or because it is the only safe way.

To conduct heat, ions must be free to move.

Sodium must be stored and handled very carefully.

A The mineral ore of aluminium

B The mineral added to the molten aluminium oxide to lower the melting point of the electrolyte

C The name for the process happening to the aluminium ions when they gain electrons

D In this electrolysis, the aluminium oxide has to be …

E Aluminium metal is produced at this electrode, often called the cathode

F The gas that is produced at the anode

G The material that the electrodes are made of; the one non-metal that conducts electricity

b Look at the word in the middle, grey column in the completed puzzle, and answer the question.

What is the chemical formula of the substance highlighted?

....

Exercise 16.3 Corrosion and rusting

IN THIS EXERCISE YOU WILL:

Science skills:

* investigate corrosion and rusting in the context of different metals.

English skills:

* learn to use phrases to connect an action and a purpose/aim.

KEY WORDS

rust: a loose, orange–brown, flaky layer of hydrated iron(III) oxide, $Fe_2O_3 \cdot xH_2O$, found on the surface of iron or steel

rusting: the corrosion of iron and steel to form rust (hydrated iron(III) oxide)

sacrificial protection: a method of rust protection involving the attachment of blocks of a metal more reactive than iron to a structure; this metal is corroded rather than the iron or steel structure

3 Circle the correct options to complete the following statements about aluminium.

Aluminium is a **light / heavy** metal and has **poor / good** electrical conductivity. It is used in the construction of aircraft, usually in the form of **mixtures / alloys** with other **metals / non-metals** such as copper. Its **low / high** density and good conductivity mean that it is used in overhead power cables.

Aluminium is particularly useful because it is resistant to **rusting / corrosion**. This makes aluminium containers useful for storing food.

Aluminium is an ideal candidate for **recycling / reusing** because making it by electrolysis is very **inexpensive / expensive**. It takes a **large / low** amount of energy to run the electrolysis cells. Recycling aluminium saves about 95% of the energy needed to make new aluminium.

4 Iron and steel objects do not form a protective layer like aluminium. In their case the iron oxide (**rust**) that is formed flakes off and the metal is eaten away.

a What two substances are needed for the rusting of an iron object to occur?

....

b In order to prevent **rusting**, objects can be coated with a protective layer. This method is called barrier protection.

    i Give two examples of materials that can be used to form this layer.

    ....

    ii Write a sentence explaining why this method is used. Include the phrase *so that*.

    ....

    ....

> LANGUAGE FOCUS
>
> When you want to describe the purpose or aim of an action, use *in order to* or *so that* to connect the action and the purpose/aim. *In order to* and *so that* mean the same thing, but different grammar is used after them.
>
> You oil a machine <u>in order to stop</u> rust from developing.
>
> You oil a machine <u>so that rusting does not</u> occur.
>
> You oil a machine <u>in order to allow it</u> to work properly.
>
> You oil a machine <u>so that it works properly</u>.
>
> *in order to* + *to* + infinitive   *so that* + subject + verb
>
> *In order to* can sometimes be shortened to *to*:
>
> You oil a machine <u>to</u> allow it to work properly.

5   a   Figure 16.2 illustrates a method of rust prevention known as **sacrificial protection**.

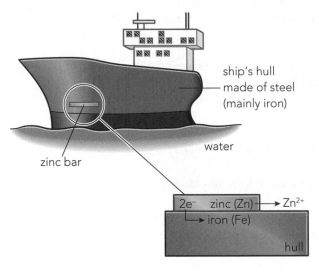

Figure 16.2: Blocks of zinc or magnesium are used for the sacrificial protection of ships' hulls.

Explain how sacrificial protection works. Use the phrase *in order to* in your explanation.

....

....

....

....

....

b   Coating an iron object with a complete layer of zinc can serve both as a form
of barrier and as sacrificial protection, depending on the circumstances.
What is the name given to this process? Explain the circumstances where this
treatment can act in the two different ways.

....

....

....

....

....

....

....

....

c   Complete the following statement about stainless steel. Use either *in order to*
or *so that* to help you finish the statement.

Stainless steel is an .... of iron that is resistant to rusting.

This metal contains iron that has been mixed with another ....

metal that does not corrode easily ....

....

Chapter 17

Chemistry of our environment

IN THIS CHAPTER YOU WILL:

Science skills:

- describe the composition of clean dry air and the nature of some atmospheric pollution problems

- understand processes involved in producing clean water for industrial and domestic use.

English skills:

- practise terminology used to describe the composition and pollution of the atmosphere

- consider how to construct a summary of an issue or topic.

Exercise 17.1 Composition of air

IN THIS EXERCISE YOU WILL:

Science skills:

- interpret data relating to the composition of clean dry air.

English skills:

- use superlatives to rank things.

KEY WORDS

atmosphere: the layer of air and water vapour surrounding the Earth

clean dry air: containing no water vapour and only the gases which are always present in the air

greenhouse gas: a gas that absorbs thermal energy reflected from the surface of the Earth, stopping it escaping the atmosphere

1   The data in Table 17.1 show the proportions of the gases found in **clean dry air**, and their boiling points.

Gas	Boiling point / °C	Proportion in mixture / %
nitrogen	−196	78
oxygen	−183	21
carbon dioxide	(sublimes)	0.04
argon	−186	0.90
krypton	−153	—*
xenon	−108	—*
helium	−249	—*
neon	−246	—*

* All the other noble gases in the air make up 0.06% of the total volume.

Carbon dioxide does not have a boiling point at atmospheric pressure as it sublimes. Sublimation is not required knowledge for this syllabus.

Table 17.1: The composition of clean dry air.

a   Identify the type of chart shown. Then, using data from Table 17.1, complete the labels for the different segments.

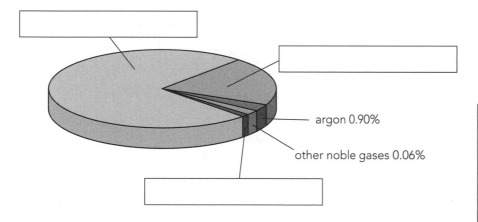

argon 0.90%

other noble gases 0.06%

Type of chart: ....

b   Give the name of the gas described in the following statements **i–vii**. Use the information in Table 17.1 to help you.

i   The most abundant gas in the **atmosphere**: ....

ii   The second most common gas in the atmosphere: ....

iii   The gas with the highest boiling point: ....

LANGUAGE TIP

You use the superlative when you rank things at the top or bottom of a list, e.g. *Osmium is the densest* metal, but you can also add ordinal numbers (*sixth, eighth*, etc.) to rank other things, e.g. *Iridium is the second densest metal. Platinum is the third densest*.

iv The gas with the lowest boiling point: ....

v The gas with the second lowest boiling point: ....

vi The most reactive gas in the atmosphere: ....

vii The most common noble gas in the atmosphere: ....

LANGUAGE FOCUS

In English, you usually put new or 'most interesting' information at the end of a sentence. Think of, for instance, competitions where you hear *The winner is... / The prize goes to...* or when you answer a question with a complete sentence:

Where did uranium get its name from?   *It got its name from the planet Uranus.*

In this example 'got its name from' is in the question; 'the planet Uranus' is new to the conversation. Similarly:

Which is the densest alkali metal?   *The densest alkali metal is caesium.*

Here are two more situations in which you put new or 'most interesting' information at the end of the sentence in chemistry:

1   When you correct something, you often move the correction to the end of the sentence, because it's the new, 'most important' information.

Carbon has atomic number 5.

'That's not correct; the element with atomic number 5 is boron.'

'Boron' is the correction; it is at the end of the sentence. 'The element with atomic number 5' is the part of the sentence that we already know; it becomes the subject of the new sentence.

2   The first sentence of a well-written paragraph or text tells you what the paragraph or text is about. Therefore, the end of the first sentence gives you the topic of the paragraph or text, because the most important information in a sentence goes at the end.

There are several gases in Earth's atmosphere, and one of them is oxygen. (= first sentence in a text about oxygen)

Everyone knows humans need oxygen, but oxygen is only one of several gases in Earth's atmosphere. (= first sentence in a text about the gases in Earth's atmosphere)

2 **a** Read the statements and put a ✓ (correct) or ✗ (incorrect) in the box.
Then correct the incorrect sentences, referring to the Language Focus box
and the example to help you.

    i Litmus paper is an indicator that turns yellow in alkaline solution. ✗

    That's not correct; an indicator that turns yellow in alkaline solution is <u>methylorange</u>.

    ii A group of unreactive elements are the noble gases. ☐

    ....

    ....

    iii In clean dry air, nitrogen is the only **greenhouse gas**. ☐

    ....

    ....

    iv The most reactive gas in the Earth's atmosphere is oxygen. ☐

    ....

    ....

    v The only gaseous compound in clean dry air is water. ☐

    ....

    ....

  b Read the five correct sentences in **2a** again. Choose the best three sentences to
begin texts with each of the following titles.

    A 'The noble gases in the air' ....

    B 'Methyl orange as an indicator' ....

    C 'Carbon dioxide' ....

  c Write a suitable first sentence for texts on each of the following topics.
Use the information in the Language Focus box to help.

    i William Ramsay, the chemist who discovered the noble gases

    ....

    ....

    ii The presence of greenhouse gases in the air

    ....

    ....

Exercise 17.2 Air quality and climate

IN THIS EXERCISE YOU WILL:

Science skills:

- consider two of the processes involved in sustaining the composition balance of the air and some of the factors that pollute it.

English skills:

- become familiar with key terms related to air quality.

KEY WORDS

combustion: a chemical reaction in which a substance reacts with oxygen – the reaction is exothermic

photosynthesis: the chemical process by which plants synthesise glucose from atmospheric carbon dioxide and water giving off oxygen as a by-product; the energy required for the process is captured from sunlight by chlorophyll molecules in the green leaves of the plants

3   Human activity has resulted in changes in the gases present in the air. There are several atmospheric problems arising from this pollution. Reorder the letters to find words related to types of pollution and the chemicals involved. Use the clues in brackets to help.

diac nari	_acid rain_	(rain with a low pH)
neathem	_methane_	(simplest hydrocarbon)
gbloa giwarnm	....	(it's getting warmer)
nzeoo aryle	....	(outer layer of the atmosphere)
fulrus dixodei	....	(an acidic gas)
htopomechcilac ogms	....	(air pollution in cities)
abcnor ddeiiox	....	(a greenhouse gas)
aceilmt aceghn	....	(a change in regional weather patterns)

4   There is a balance which maintains the levels of carbon dioxide and oxygen in the air. Some processes use up these atmospheric gases, whereas others produce them. Two of the processes involved in keeping the balance are **combustion** on the one hand, and **photosynthesis** on the other.

a In the spaces provided, write the correct word for the process that each picture shows.

i .... ii ....

b Write definitions of the two processes shown in the pictures in part **a**. Use some of the words from this word pool and your own ideas.

carbon dioxide   energy   fossil fuels   glucose

green   leaves   oxygen   obtained   process   plants

produced   reaction   Sun   uses   wood

i The process in the first picture is called ....

It is ....

....

ii The process in the second picture is called ....

It is ....

....

Exercise 17.3 Clean water for domestic use

IN THIS EXERCISE YOU WILL:

Science skills:

* understand the steps in the water purification process and the importance of clean drinking water.

English skills:

* consider the structure of a written analysis, and how to write a good introductory paragraph.

KEY WORD

filtration: the separation of a solid from a liquid, using a fine filter paper which does not allow the solid to pass through

5 Figure 17.1 shows steps in one type of water purification process.

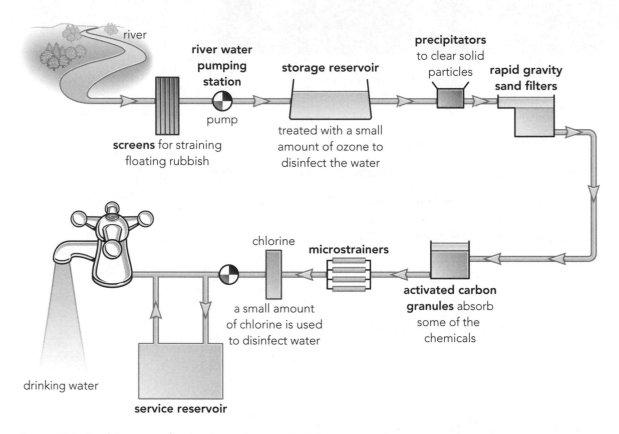

Figure 17.1: Purifying water for the domestic water supply.

a Which two chemicals are used to disinfect the water?

....

b What is killed in the process of disinfection? Why is disinfecting the water important?

....

....

c Which two steps in the process use the separation method of **filtration**?

....

d What do the activated carbon (charcoal) granules do? Tick the correct box.

Attach some chemicals to themselves, removing them from the water. ☐

Turn some chemicals into other, harmless, substances. ☐

Cause harmful chemicals to coagulate (stick together) with each other. ☐

6 Some important terms concerned with water purification are listed below (some are used in Figure 17.1). Complete the definitions **a–e** using the terms given.

break down   precipitator   pesticide   reservoir   absorb

a .... : to split harmful chemical compounds into simpler
harmless substances

b .... : a chemical which kills insects that harm crops

c .... : an action where harmful chemicals are removed from the
water by attachment to a powder (e.g. activated carbon)

d .... : a chemical is added which causes very small, insoluble
particles to stick together and fall to the bottom of
the container

e .... : a large tank or container for storing large amounts
of water

LANGUAGE FOCUS

When you write an analysis, you start with an introductory paragraph. A good introductory paragraph can be quite short (three or four sentences) but should be well structured and clear, so that the reader is immediately interested, understands what the text is about and wants to keep reading. Here are the three things to include.

1 A topic sentence – the first sentence with the main topic identified in the last words of the sentence:

Carbon dioxide is one of the most powerful greenhouse gases in our air.

2 A middle sentence or two that give a general view or a definition of the topic identified in the topic sentence:

Greenhouse gases are gases that absorb thermal energy reflected from the Earth, preventing it escaping into space.

3 A final sentence that gives a reason for the analysis:

At the moment, the world's environment is threatened by rising global temperature, so it is important to look at reducing the production of greenhouse gases.

LANGUAGE TIP

Analyse can be a command word, as well as being used to refer to chemical analysis. As a command word, *analyse* requires you to examine something in detail to show meaning, identify the main points and show the relationship between them.

7　**a**　Salma has written an analysis of the need for clean water. Put her paragraphs in the correct order by writing a number (**1–4**) in the boxes. Read the Language Focus box again to help you.

> We have many uses for water, including agricultural, industrial and sports activities. Most of these require fresh water. It has been estimated that 70% of water use worldwide is for agriculture. However, the area of life with a crucial need for clean water is in the home. Clean water at home is essential for health, as water that is not clean often causes fatal diseases. Furthermore, in some parts of the world, it is considered a girl's job to walk long distances to fetch the family's water. This means those girls do not have time to go to school. ☐
>
> Three-quarters of our world is covered in water. However, only 2.5% of water on Earth is fresh water, and over 65% of this is frozen in glaciers and the ice caps of the north and south poles. The increase in human population means that competition for this water is growing and underground sources are being used up. ☐
>
> In conclusion, scientists and engineers need to invent cheap and practical ways of supplying clean water for towns and villages in areas where it is not currently available. Achieving this will improve the life expectancy and quality of a great proportion of the world's population. ☐
>
> Water supply for human use is threatened in various ways. Changes in weather patterns due to climate change will have an impact on water supply, particularly in regions with reduced rainfall. Many pollutants also threaten water supplies. Some of these pollutants come from industry and agriculture, and include heavy metals, acidic or alkaline chemicals, and pesticides. ☐

b　Salma wants to end each of her paragraphs with one of the following sentences **A–D**. Write the paragraph number (**1–4**) after each sentence.

A　Providing clean drinking water to as many people as possible should be a universal goal. ☐

B　Therefore, introducing a sanitised water supply to a town or village can improve health and free up time for education, having a positive impact on girls' lives. ☐

C　Water is essential to life and to many human activities, but it is unequally distributed around the world. ☐

D　Perhaps the most frequent and dangerous water pollution in streams and rivers comes from raw sewage pumped from homes nearby. ☐

c   Look at Salma's introductory paragraph. Copy the correct words or
    sentences. Use the numbered points in the Language Focus box to help you.

    i   The topic sentence:

    ....

    ii   The word(s) that tell us the topic of her analysis:

    ....

    iii A general view or definition of the topic:

    ....

    iv   The reason for the analysis:

    ....

    ....

    ....

d   Tick (✓) the box to indicate which title would be the best for Salma's analysis.

    •   The importance of water   ☐

    •   The goal of providing a clean water supply universally   ☐

    •   Clean water for all   ☐

    Give reasons for your choice.

    ....

    ....

8   You have been asked to analyse the use of sand/carbon for the purification of
    water for the domestic supply. Write an introductory paragraph (three sentences)
    for your analysis.

    ....

    ....

    ....

    ....

    ....

    ....

> Chapter 18

Introduction to organic chemistry

IN THIS CHAPTER YOU WILL:

Science skills:

- understand how carbon can form many different compounds that can be grouped in families (homologous series)

- understand how different series of carbon compounds are named systematically.

English skills:

- meet and practise the prefixes and suffixes used in naming organic compounds

- consider how linking words can be used to connect similar ideas in a sentence.

Exercise 18.1 Naming organic compounds

IN THIS EXERCISE YOU WILL:

Science skills:

- investigate the basis for the naming of simple organic compounds (hydrocarbons).

English skills:

- see how prefixes are used in the naming of organic compounds.

KEY WORDS

alkanes: a series of hydrocarbons with the general formula C_nH_{2n+2}; they are saturated compounds as they have only single bonds between carbon atoms in their structure

displayed formula: a representation of the structure of a compound which shows all the atoms and bonds in the molecule

hydrocarbons: organic compounds which contain carbon and hydrogen only; the alkanes and alkenes are two series of hydrocarbons

saturated hydrocarbons: hydrocarbon molecules in which all the carbon–carbon bonds are single covalent bonds

The simplest organic compounds are the **hydrocarbons**, which contain carbon and hydrogen only (see Figure 18.1).

Figure 18.1: A hydrocarbon molecule with 14 carbon atoms in a straight chain.

The names of these hydrocarbons are made of two parts:

*   a prefix that tells you how many carbon atoms are in the chain (or carbon backbone) (see Table 18.1)

*   an ending (or suffix) that tells you the family of hydrocarbons they belong to (see also Exercise 18.2).

> ## LANGUAGE FOCUS
>
> In organic chemistry, the prefix of a name can tell you how many carbon atoms are in the carbon backbone of the molecule.
>
> Table 18.1 gives the prefixes and the number of carbon atoms. The prefixes marked ** are only used for these numbers in naming organic compounds. For other prefixes indicating number, see Chapter 2.
>
> The prefixes *pent-*, *hex-*, etc., are sometimes used in other areas, such as mathematics.
>
> The <u>Pent</u>agon is a building with five sides.
>
> The cells in a bee's honeycomb are <u>hex</u>agonal – they have six sides.
>
> An <u>oct</u>opus has eight legs.

> ## LANGUAGE TIP
>
> Remember that, as seen in Chapter 3, covalent bonds are bonds made between atoms by the sharing of outer electrons. Carbons are distinctive, in that they form chains and multiple bonds.

Number of carbons	Prefix	Number of carbons	Prefix
1**	meth-	6	hex-
2**	eth-	7	hept-
3**	prop-	8	oct-
4**	but-	9	non-
5	pent-	10	dec-

Table 18.1: The prefixes used in naming hydrocarbon chains.

The suffix at the end of the name for each of these straight chain hydrocarbon molecules is -*ane* and the family is the **alkanes**. In the molecules of the alkanes, all the carbon atoms are joined by single covalent bonds. The molecules are said to be saturated, because nothing can be added to them. Figure 18.2 shows the structures of the first four members of the alkane family of hydrocarbons with their names and **displayed formulae**.

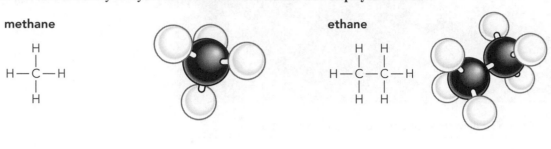

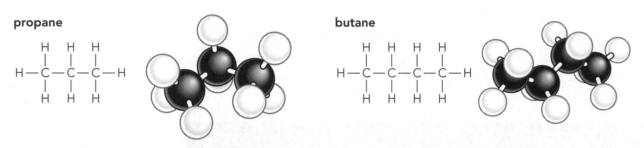

Figure 18.2: The first four **saturated hydrocarbon** molecules.

1 **a** Write the names of the following hydrocarbons, using the information given.

    i The second member of the alkane series: ....*ethane*.....

    ii The third member of the alkane series: ....

    iii The member of the alkane series with a backbone of six carbon atoms in the chain: ....

    iv The alkane with eight carbon atoms in a chain: ....

  b Give the molecular formulae of the following alkanes, using information from Figure 18.2 and Table 18.1.

    i methane: ....CH_4.......

    ii propane: ....

    iii butane: ....

    iv pentane: ....

  c All the members of the alkane series can be represented by one of these general formulae, where n = the number of carbon atoms in the chain. Circle the correct formula.

    C_nH_{2n} C_nH_{2n+1} $C_nH_{2n+1}OH$ C_nH_{2n+2}

2 Complete these sentence halves using information from question **1**.
Then draw lines to match the sentence halves together so they make five
statements about hydrocarbons.

Hydrocarbons are …	… is ………………, CH_4.
The simplest hydrocarbon …	… butane.
The major source of hydrocarbons …	… because they only contain carbon–carbon single bonds.
Alkanes are …………………… hydrocarbons …	… compounds that contain carbon and ………………… only.
The fourth member of the alkanes is …	… is the fossil fuel ……………………

Exercise 18.2 Families of organic compounds

KEY WORDS

alcohols: a series of organic compounds containing the functional group –OH and with the general formula $C_nH_{2n+1}OH$

alkenes: a series of hydrocarbons with the general formula C_nH_{2n}; they are unsaturated molecules as they have a C=C double bond somewhere in the chain.

carboxylic acids: a homologous series of organic compounds containing the functional group –COOH (–CO_2H), with the general formula $C_nH_{2n+1}COOH$

homologous series: a family of similar compounds with similar chemical properties due to the presence of the same functional group

unsaturated hydrocarbons: hydrocarbons whose molecules contain at least one carbon–carbon double or triple bond

There are several families of hydrocarbons. Alk<u>anes</u> are saturated hydrocarbons, because no more hydrogen can be added to them. However, **alk<u>enes</u>** are **unsaturated hydrocarbons**, because they contain at least one double bond in their structure (see Figure 18.3).

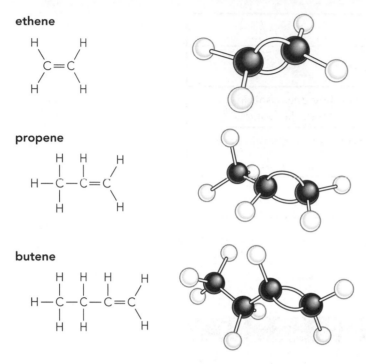

ethene

propene

butene

Figure 18.3: The first members of the alkene series.

The presence of the double bond means they can react with more hydrogen.

$$\text{alkene} + \text{hydrogen} \rightarrow \text{alkane}$$

unsaturated   *saturated*

Other **homologous series** of organic compounds occur when other atoms or groups replace a hydrogen atom in a hydrocarbon chain. The names of these different series have specific suffixes to distinguish them.

LANGUAGE FOCUS

As we saw in Chapter 4 (Exercise 4.1), the end of the name of a chemical compound can give you information about that compound. In organic chemistry, the naming is very systematic and is linked to the series of compounds involved:

-ane   the alkanes (saturated hydrocarbons, all C–C single bonds), e.g. <u>meth</u>ane, CH_4

-ene   the alkenes (unsaturated hydrocarbons with a C=C double bond), e.g. <u>eth</u>ene, C_2H_4

-ol   the **alcohols** (contain an –OH group attached to the chain), e.g. <u>meth</u>anol, CH_3OH

CONTINUED

-oic acid   the **carboxylic acids** (contain a –COOH group attached to the chain), e.g. *methanoic acid*, HCOOH (note that the C atom of the acid group counts as part of the chain)

You can see from the examples above that the appropriate prefixes (underlined) are combined with the 'family suffix' to give the compound name.

Notice also that *-an-* can be added in before the suffix to indicate that the compound is built on an alkane backbone (and this also helps with pronunciation), e.g. *methanol*, *ethanoic acid*.

The skeleton of a name of an organic compound is: prefix + (*an*) + suffix.

3   a   Complete the table with the parts of the organic name of each compound and which homologous series the compound belongs to.

Compound	Prefix	Number of carbon atoms in chain	Suffix	Homologous series
hexane	hex–	6	–ane	alkanes
butene				
ethanol				
pentanol				
ethanoic acid				

b   What are the names and chemical formulae of the following compounds?

i   The simplest alcohol: ....

ii   The simplest alkene: ....

iii   The carboxylic acid with two carbons in the backbone:

....

Exercise 18.3 General features of different organic compounds

IN THIS EXERCISE YOU WILL:

Science skills:

* learn some of the features of different types of organic compound.

English skills:

* develop the use of linking words to connect ideas.

LANGUAGE FOCUS

The most frequent linker used to connect similar ideas in a sentence is *and*:

Graphite <u>and</u> diamond are two different forms of carbon.
(= the two things are related)

Read the sentences <u>and</u> decide if they are about carbon or not.
(= you do the two things)

However, there are other linkers that you can use instead of *and* to make your writing style more scientific and interesting to read: *as well as, in addition to, furthermore, also.*

Look how you can rewrite the following sentence using these linkers:

Carbon is a solid and a non-metal.

<u>As well as</u> being a solid, carbon is a non-metal.

<u>In addition to</u> carbon being solid, it is a non-metal.

Carbon is a solid, <u>as well as</u> being a non-metal.

Carbon is a solid <u>in addition to</u> being a non-metal.

Carbon atoms form a solid. <u>Furthermore</u>, carbon is a non-metal.

Carbon is a solid. It is <u>also</u> a non-metal.

As well as and *in addition to* work in similar ways, and can be at the start or in the middle of a sentence. They do not have a subject + verb structure after them.

Furthermore comes at the start of a second sentence and you put a comma after it.

Also goes after *be* or *can*, but in front of most verbs. It is generally near the beginning of a sentence.

Diamonds are <u>also</u> made of carbon atoms.

Diamonds <u>also</u> have a structure made of carbon atoms.

4   a   Match the following sentence halves **A–C** and **1–3** to make complete sentences, then write the letter + number combinations on the lines in **i–iii**.

A	In addition to the ability to form long chains, …
B	Alkanes are compounds containing only carbon and hydrogen, …
C	Ethanol is flammable …

1	… as well as being a colourless liquid.
2	… carbon atoms can also form multiple bonds with each other.
3	… and all the bonds between carbon atoms are single bonds.

Then write out each sentence in the space provided, circling the linkers of addition in the sentence halves.

i   The sentence that explains why there are so many carbon compounds:

   .... + ...

   ....

   ....

ii   The sentence that describes two properties of ethanol:

   .... + ...

   ....

   ....

iii The sentence that describes the molecules of alkanes:

   .... + ...

   ....

   ....

b   Complete the following sentences, using the linkers below. More than one answer may be possible.

   also   and   as well as   furthermore   in addition

i   .... to being colourless gases, the short chain alkanes .... burn very easily.

ii   Ethanol is a neutral liquid, ... being a useful solvent.

iii Methane is a major component of natural gas. ...., it is .... an important greenhouse gas.

iv   The alcohols are useful as solvents. ...., they burn easily .... are used as fuels.

c   Complete the following sentences using the linkers from the Language Focus box.

i   Unlike alkanes containing carbon and hydrogen atoms, alcohol and carboxylic acid molecules ....

   ....

ii   Pentene molecules contain a carbon–carbon double bond ....

   ....

iii Carbon can exist in the form of graphite. ...., it ....

   ....

Chapter 19

Reactions of organic compounds

IN THIS CHAPTER YOU WILL:

Science skills:

- understand that organic compounds can show isomerism, with molecules having the same molecular formula but different structures

- describe and contrast the different methods of ethanol production.

English skills:

- work with the terms used in describing the properties of different groups of organic compounds

- contrast different ideas and processes using both, each and various linkers.

Exercise 19.1 Alkanes and alkenes

IN THIS EXERCISE YOU WILL:

Science skills:

- consider how alkanes and alkenes take part in different types of chemical reaction: substitution reactions and addition reactions.

English skills:

- practise discussing features shared by alkanes and alkenes, and vocabulary used in this chapter.

KEY WORDS

addition reaction: a reaction in which a simple molecule adds across the carbon–carbon double bond of an alkene

Alkanes and alkenes are both hydrocarbons made from the elements carbon and hydrogen. Alkenes are more reactive because they have a carbon–carbon double bond in their structure. They take part in **addition reactions**, such as the addition reaction with hydrogen (see Exercise 18.2). The addition reaction with bromine water can be used as a test for alkenes.

1   Complete the puzzle about hydrocarbons using the clues given.

						B					
A						B					
B						A					
C						C					
D						K					
E						B					
F						O					
G						N					
H						E					

A   One of the two elements that make up hydrocarbons.

B   Some hydrocarbons are …, because they only contain single carbon–carbon bonds.

C   A hydrocarbon with ten carbon atoms and no double bonds.

D   The name of the alcohol containing four carbon atoms.

E   The fraction from the distillation of petroleum used to surface roads.

F   The type of bonding in all hydrocarbons.

G   The alcohol made by reacting ethene with steam.

H   The general name for hydrocarbons with a double bond.

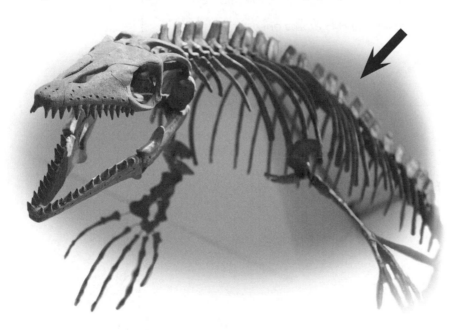

Figure 19.1: Dinosaur fossil skeleton highlighting its backbone.

LANGUAGE TIP

When you meet new words in English, try forming a fun, visual association with the words to help you learn them. For example, imagine a dinosaur when you think of the hydrocarbon backbone in organic molecules.

LANGUAGE FOCUS

When expressing similarity between things, you can use words such as *each* or *both*.

Each emphasises that separate but similar things share a characteristic:

<u>*Each element*</u> *in the Periodic Table has an atomic number.*

There are 118 known elements, and <u>*each (one)*</u> *has a symbol.*

There are 118 known elements, and <u>*each of them*</u> *has a symbol.*

Remember: *both* expresses similarity between <u>two</u> things, but not more than two (Chapter 3):

<u>*Both*</u> *the dinosaur fossil and the hydrocarbon molecule consist of a chain of units.*

<u>*Both (of the)*</u> *backbones consist of a chain of units.*

<u>*Both (of them)*</u> *consist of a chain of units.*

Notice that *both* goes in front of *and*, but *each* goes after *and*.

Also notice that *both* + subject uses a plural verb, but *each* + subject uses a singular verb.

Dalton and Rutherford were scientists. <u>*Both*</u> *are famous in the field of atomic theory.*

<u>*Each*</u> *of them is famous in the field of atomic theory.*

To express difference, use *whereas*. It is like *but*, but is only used to contrast two opposite things. It goes at the start of a sentence, or in the middle:

<u>*Whereas*</u> *hydrocarbon molecules contain C and H atoms only, alcohols also contain O atoms.*

Hydrocarbon molecules contain C and H atoms only, <u>*whereas*</u> *alcohols also contain O atoms.*

---

2 a Read this information and answer the question. Then complete statements **i–v** using *both* or *each*. These statements explain why the answer is true.

The word highlighted in the puzzle in question **1** is the same for both the part of the fossil indicated in Figure 19.1 and a feature of a hydrocarbon molecule. Why?

....

....

Because:

i .... of them consists of repeating structures.

ii .... has a structure made up of repeating units.

iii .... have structures made up of repeating units.

iv .... one of them is made up of a series of repeating units.

v .... the dinosaur fossil and the hydrocarbon molecule are based on a repeating structure.

b Circle the correct option in the following sentences.

  i **Each / Both / Whereas** alkanes and alkenes contain only carbon and hydrogen atoms.

  ii **Each / Both / Whereas** alkane or alkene molecule contains only carbon and hydrogen atoms.

  iii Alkane and alkene molecules **each / both / whereas** contain only carbon and hydrogen atoms.

  iv An alkane molecule contains only carbon–carbon single bonds, **each / both / whereas** an alkene contains at least one double bond.

  v **Each / Both / Whereas** an alkane contains only carbon–carbon single bonds, an alkene has at least one double bond.

c Write complete sentences using *both*, *each* or *whereas* on the following topics.

  i The hydrocarbons that are saturated and the hydrocarbons that are unsaturated

    ....

    ....

  ii The fact that ethane and propane are alkanes, but they have different numbers of carbon atoms

    ....

    ....

d What is the general name of the group of atoms attached to the backbone of an organic molecule that gives the molecule its characteristic properties?

....

Give an example of one of these groups. ....

3 A simple chemical test can be used to decide whether a compound is an alkene or an alkane. The test gives a positive reaction for alk<u>enes</u>. Complete the following paragraph describing the test, using the words given. There is one word you do not need.

colourless   ethene   orange   reaction   saturated

unsaturated   water

If .... gas is bubbled into a solution of bromine ....,

then the orange solution turns .... This test is positive for all

.... hydrocarbons.

However, if ethane gas is bubbled into bromine water, there is no ....

The solution stays ....

LANGUAGE TIP

A solution is *clear* when you can see through it easily, but it may be coloured, e.g. copper(II) sulfate solution is *clear* and blue. A *colourless* liquid, e.g. ethanol, or solution has no colour.

Exercise 19.2 Isomerism and molecular structure

IN THIS EXERCISE YOU WILL:

Science skills:

- consider how the different organic molecules can have the same molecular formula but different structures.

English skills:

- develop the systematic naming of organic compounds and the naming of isomers.

KEY WORD

isomers: compounds which have the same molecular formula but different structural arrangements of the atoms – they have different structural formulae

4 There are more compounds of carbon than of any other element. Part of the reason is that the carbon atoms in a molecule do not all have to be in the backbone. Some can be part of branches off the main chain (see Figure 19.2). These are called branched chain molecules.

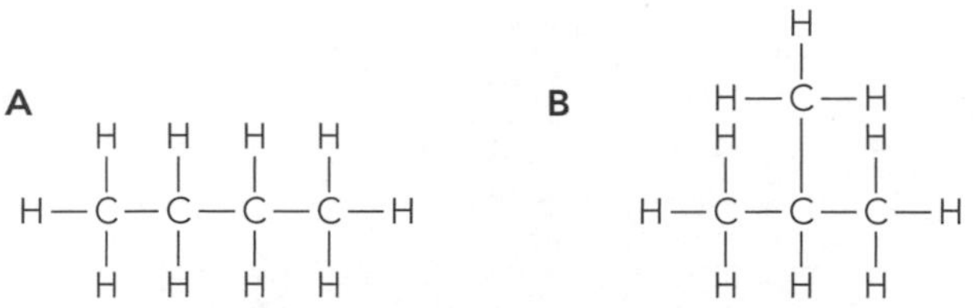

Figure 19.2: Examples of straight and branched chain alkanes.

a What is the name of hydrocarbon **A** in Figure 19.2? It has the molecular formula C_4H_{10}. ....

b How many carbon atoms are there in the longest chain in molecule **B** in Figure 19.2? ....
This hydrocarbon has a name based on propane. It is called methylpropane.

c A molecular formula tells you the numbers of atoms of each element in a molecule of the compound. What is the molecular formula of methylpropane? ....
The hydrocarbons **A** and **B** in Figure 19.2 are different compounds, despite having the same molecular formula. They are **isomers** of each other; **A** has the structural formula $CH_3CH_2CH_2CH_3$. What is the structural formula of **B**?

....

d Complete the following statement about isomers using the words below.

compounds **isomerism** **same** **structures**

Isomers are .... with the .... molecular formula but different .... This property is known as ....

e Read the following information and answer the question.
Both structures in Figure 19.3 are alkenes and both have the formula C_4H_8. They are isomers of each other, with the double bond in different positions in the hydrocarbon backbone.

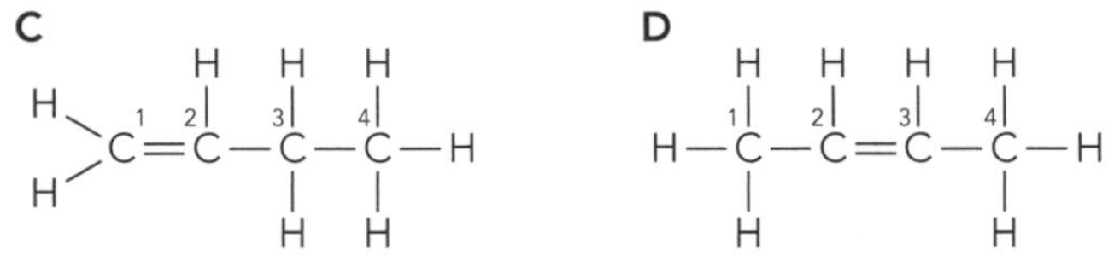

Figure 19.3: Displayed formulae of two alkene isomers.

Hydrocarbon **C** is known as but-1-ene because:

- it has four carbons in the chain, and
- the double bond starts at the first carbon atom in the chain.

What is hydrocarbon **D** called? ....

LANGUAGE TIP

Despite is similar to *but*, but it emphasises an unexpected or atypical element in a situation. Use it before a noun or *-ing* word: *Despite being sunny, it is cold. / It is cold, despite the sunshine.*

5 Find and circle 13 words related to organic chemistry in the word puzzle, then use them to complete the sentences and definitions.

H	O	M	O	L	O	G	O	U	S	F	R
P	R	O	E	A	V	C	T	F	I	U	S
L	F	N	E	T	H	E	N	E	N	N	T
V	A	O	G	P	H	W	E	H	G	C	R
P	K	M	L	O	I	A	J	S	L	T	U
E	J	E	A	L	K	A	N	E	E	I	C
T	O	R	H	Y	G	P	R	E	Z	O	T
H	I	S	O	M	E	R	I	S	M	N	U
A	H	S	D	E	R	L	X	N	D	A	R
N	R	Y	C	R	N	O	E	O	I	L	A
O	B	S	A	T	U	R	A	T	E	D	L
L	X	V	L	C	O	V	A	L	E	N	T

A   The name given to a 'family' of organic compounds:

an .... series

B   The type of bonding in organic compounds: ....

C   The simplest hydrocarbon of all: ....

D   **C** is the simplest member of this 'family' of hydrocarbons:

....

E and F   The molecules of this 'family' contain only ....

carbon–carbon bonds. They are said to be ....

hydrocarbons.

G   The simplest hydrocarbon containing a carbon–carbon double bond:

....

H   The second of the series of alcohols produced by fermentation of

sugars using yeast: ....

I   The group that is responsible for the characteristic properties of a

'family' of compounds is called a .... group.

J   Two formulas can be written for each organic compound; one is the

molecular formula, the other is the .... formula.

K   When two compounds have the same molecular formula but different

          structures, it is called ....

L and M   Compounds such as **G** above can react with each other to form a

          long chain molecule called a .... The individual small

          molecules are called ....

Exercise 19.3 Alcohols and acids

IN THIS EXERCISE YOU WILL:

Science skills:

- investigate alcohols and organic acids.

English skills:

- become familiar with some key terms related to alcohols and organic acids.

KEY WORDS

fermentation: a reaction carried out using a living organism, usually a yeast or bacteria, to produce a useful chemical compound; usually refers to the production of ethanol

hydration: the addition of the elements of water across a carbon–carbon double bond: H– adds to one carbon, and –OH to the other

6   The alcohol functional group is –OH. The acid functional group is –COOH. Write the name and formula for the alcohols and acids. Remember: the carbon in the acid group counts as part of the chain when naming the acid.

a   The straight chain alcohol with four carbon atoms is .... and its

    formula is ....

b   The carboxylic acid with three carbon atoms in the chain is ....

    and its formula is ....

7 The two methods of producing ethanol are:

- the **hydration** of ethene (addition of water)
- the **fermentation** of glucose-containing material using yeast.

Each method has its advantages and disadvantages. The method chosen will depend on the availability of resources and on the main reason for producing the ethanol. A comparison of the methods is summarised in Table 19.1.

Ethanol by hydration of ethene	Ethanol by fermentation
originates from a non-renewable resource – petroleum	made from a readily renewable resource
small-scale equipment capable of withstanding pressure	relatively simple large-scale vessels
a continuous process	a batch process – need to start process again each time
a fast reaction rate	a relatively slow process
yields highly pure ethanol	ethanol must be purified by distillation – though the fermentation product can sometimes be used immediately for some purposes
a sophisticated complex method	a simple, straightforward method

Table 19.1: A comparison of the industrial methods of ethanol production.

LANGUAGE FOCUS

To contrast two ideas in a sentence, you are already familiar with *but* and *whereas*. However, in science, using different linkers of contrast, like *however*, *although* and *despite*, will improve your writing style.

However can usually replace *but*, but you should put it at the start of a new sentence:

Using a Bunsen burner may seem safe. <u>However</u>, remember to wear safety glasses.

Use *although* when the truth is possibly unexpected, or to give a warning:

<u>Although</u> magnesium sulfate looks like sugar, do not put it in your tea. (= warning)

Carbon dioxide can be poured from a tube, <u>although</u> it is a gas. (= pouring gas is unexpected)

Notice: *although* can start the sentence or go in the middle, after a comma.

Despite has the same meaning as *although*, but you cannot use a subject + verb structure after it. Use a noun or *-ing* word and then a comma or full stop:

<u>Despite</u> looking like sugar, do not put magnesium sulfate in your tea.

Carbon dioxide can be poured from a tube, <u>despite</u> being a gas.

a Complete the sentences using the linkers below to compare the methods of ethanol production.

although   despite   however   whereas

i .... using non-renewable resources, the production of ethanol by hydration of ethene is still used.

ii .... fermentation produces ethanol, it is not pure, and the product must be distilled to purify it.

iii The hydration of ethene with steam produces pure ethanol.

........................, the equipment and process are expensive to run.

iv Production of ethanol by fermentation is a simple, straightforward method, ... the hydration of ethene is sophisticated and complex.

b Answer the following questions. Include the linkers in the Language Focus box.

i What is the difference in the number of products produced by substitution and addition reactions? Is the reaction between ethene and steam a substitution or an addition reaction?

....

....

....

....

....

....

ii What is the difference between a renewable and a non-renewable resource?

....

....

....

Petrochemicals and polymers

Exercise 20.1 Petrochemicals

KEY WORDS

fractions (from distillation): the different mixtures that distil over at different temperatures during fractional distillation

petroleum (or crude oil): a fossil fuel formed underground over many millions of years by conditions of high pressure and temperature acting on the remains of dead sea creatures

1   **Petroleum** is a natural resource containing many different hydrocarbons of varying chain lengths and boiling points. The hydrocarbons can be separated by **fractional distillation** (see Figure 20.1).

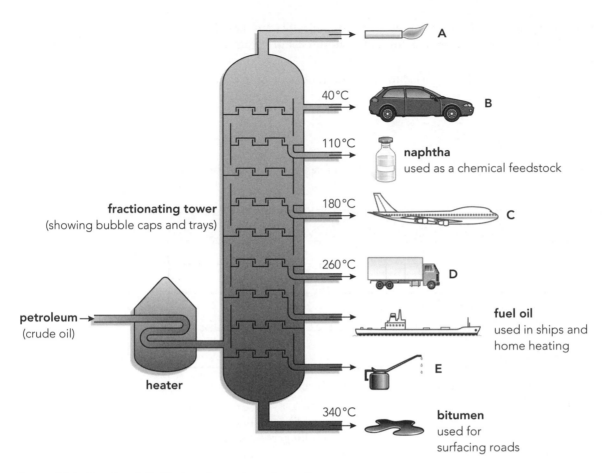

Figure 20.1: Fractional distillation of petroleum in a refinery.

a   Match the terms below to fractions **A–E** in Figure 20.1.

   diesel oil   lubricating oil   paraffin (kerosene)

   petrol (gasoline)   refinery gas

   A   ....

   B   ....

   C   ....

   D   ....

   E   ....

b   Identify which fraction **A–E** contains hydrocarbons with the lowest boiling
   point. ....

c   Identify which fraction **A–E** contains the longest hydrocarbon
   molecules. ....

2 The long-chain hydrocarbons are less important economically than the others. These long-chain molecules are broken down into shorter chains by the process of cracking.

    a The following reaction is often used to illustrate cracking. Complete the word equation.

$$C_{10}H_{22} \xrightarrow{\text{heat and catalyst}} C_8H_{18} \quad + \quad C_2H_4$$

decane   →   .... + ...

    b Complete the table comparing decane to the gas formed in the reaction in part **a**.

	Decane (a liquid)	.... (a gas)
Hydrocarbon series	alkane	alkene
Saturated or unsaturated?	....	....
Reacts with bromine water? Yes/No	....	....
Boiling point above/below room temperature	....	....

    c Complete the following statement about cracking by circling the correct choice of words.

       Cracking is a reaction in which a **long- / short-** chain alkane is broken down using heat and a catalyst. The products are usually a **longer- / shorter-** chain **alkene / alkane** and a **short- / long-** chain alkene.

LANGUAGE FOCUS

Acid rain causes increased rusting of iron objects. Acid rain is a **cause**, and the increased rusting is an effect or consequence. When you want to link a cause with its effect or result, you can use the words *so* and *because*. Sometimes, instead of *so*, you can use *Consequently* or *Therefore*.

Because begins the part of the sentence that expresses a cause:

Increased rusting occurs with acid rain <u>because</u> it has a high concentration of dissolved ions.
          effect/result   cause

Consequently, *Therefore* and *so* begin the part of the sentence that expresses an effect:

Acid rain has a high concentration of dissolved ions. <u>Consequently/Therefore</u>, it causes more rusting.
          cause   effect/result

Acid rain has a high concentration of dissolved ions, <u>so</u> more rusting occurs.
          cause   effect/result

Notice where the commas or full stops are placed.

d Complete the following sentences using the correct word in brackets.

   i Alkanes are saturated hydrocarbons. ...., they cannot take part in addition reactions. (*Because* / *Consequently*)

   ii Aluminium has a lower density than steel. ...., aluminium is used rather than steel when building aircraft. (*So* / *Therefore*)

   iii .... various types of plastic are light and resistant to chemical attack, they are very useful for storing food. (*Because* / *Therefore*)

   iv Carbon dioxide is a greenhouse gas, ...we need to reduce the level of carbon dioxide emissions produced by our activities. (*because* / *so*)

   v Plastic containers are used for storage .... they are strong, light and resistant to corrosion. (*because* / *therefore*)

   vi Acids react with many metals. ...., many metals corrode in contact with acidic solutions. (*consequently* / *so*)

e Complete the following sentences using the word in brackets.

   i The alkali metals all react with oxygen and water vapour in the air.

   ...., ...

   (*consequently*)

   ii .... litmus ....,

   it can be used as an acid–base indicator. (*because*)

   iii Alkanes and alkenes react differently with bromine water,

   ....

   .... (*so*)

   iv The electronic configurations of noble gas atoms are very stable.

   ....

   .... (*therefore*)

Exercise 20.2 Polymers and plastics

IN THIS EXERCISE YOU WILL:

Science skills:

- investigate two different types of polymerisation reaction and the usefulness of the products made.

English skills:

- look at how different types of polymers are named.

KEY WORDS

monomer: a small molecule, such as ethene, which can be polymerised to make a polymer

polymer: a substance consisting of very large molecules made by polymerising a large number of repeating units or monomers

polymerisation: the chemical reaction in which molecules (monomers) join together to form a long-chain polymer

3 Ethene can be used to make a **polymer** called poly(ethene) in an addition reaction (see Figure 20.2). Notice how poly(ethene) is named: the name of the monomer *ethene* is in brackets, with the prefix poly- before it.

ethene $\xrightarrow[\text{heat, catalyst}]{\text{high pressure}}$ poly(ethene)

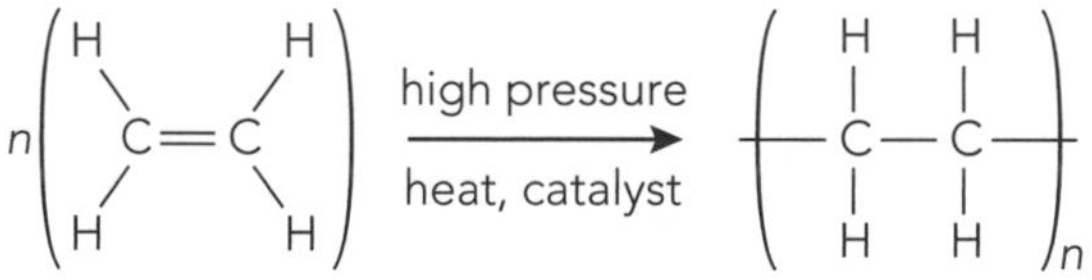

Figure 20.2: Addition **polymerisation** of ethene; a very large number of **monomers** (*n*) are joined together.

LANGUAGE TIP

Remember, the prefix *mono-* means 'one/single'. You find it in words like *monomer*. *poly-* means 'many/multiple'; it is found in words like *polyglot*, *polygon* and many words related to *polymers*.

Give the names of the monomers and polymers in the table.

Monomer		Polymer
ethene	CH_2=CH_2	poly(ethene)
....	CH_2=$CHCH_3$	poly(propene)
styrene	CH_2=CHC_6H_5	....
chloroethene	CH_2=$CHCl$	....

Some of the questions in Exercises 20.1 and 20.2 use the command words *consider* and *identify*. *Consider* means to review and respond to the given information. *Identify* means to name/select/recognise the correct option.

Other important command words include the following:

Deduce: conclude from available information

Demonstrate: show how to do something or give an example

Examine: investigate something closely, in detail

Justify: support your case with evidence or argument

Predict: suggest what may happen based on available information

Suggest: apply knowledge and understanding to situations where there are a range of valid responses in order to make proposals / put forward considerations

4   Read this passage about polymers and circle the correct options.

Condensation / Addition polymerisation occurs when two **monomers / polymers** react to form a polymer and another simple product. Each time a link is **broken / made**, a water molecule is produced. **Poly(ethene) / Nylon** and PET are examples of this type of polymerisation. **Proteins / Fatty acids** are natural polymers made by the same polymerisation process.

Because addition **monomers / polymers** are **synthetic / natural**, there are no **natural / artificial** ways of breaking them down. Polymers of this type are said to be **biodegradable / non-biodegradable**.

Exercise 20.3 The use of plastics

IN THIS EXERCISE YOU WILL:

Science skills:

*   consider the advantages and disadvantages of the use of plastics.

English skills:

*   learn how to structure a discussion and justify your argument.

KEY WORD

plastics: polymers that can be moulded or shaped by the action of heat and pressure

---

LANGUAGE FOCUS

When discussing controversial issues like the use of polymers in packaging or of hydrogen as a fuel, be careful to structure your analysis of the debate carefully. One way of doing this is to divide your analysis into four parts:

1   Introduction (see Chapter 17)

2   Advantages

3   Disadvantages (Chapters 18 and 19 can help you with linkers)

4   Conclusion (see Chapter 15)

The conclusions paragraph can be quite short. It should show your opinion on the issue and your reasons, and if you think the advantages or the disadvantages are more important. It often gives a suggestion for future action or change. For example:

In conclusion, the use of polymers in packaging has brought us great advantages. However, developing systems of re-use and recycling still challenges us technologically. <u>Therefore, in order to protect our environment, we urgently need to change our habit of disposing so much plastic before it is too late.</u>

The last sentence of any conclusions paragraph is very important. It often consists of a positive prediction or a warning, includes 'we' and invites the reader to think and agree.

For example:

Let us hope these future developments improve the environment.

If we do not take action soon, the future could bring many environmental problems.

---

5   Write your own final sentence for a report on each of the following issues.

    a   The mining of the ocean floor for rare metals

        ....

        ....

        ....

        ....

    b   Continuing to clear large areas of tropical rainforest for towns and ranching

        ....

        ....

        ....

        ....

6   Chidi has written an analysis on the use of hydrogen as a fuel. Look at his notes and use them to write his conclusions paragraph.

> Hydrogen – much higher energy output than other fuels – environmentally clean – only product – water vapour. Storage and distribution will need to be safe – highly explosive. Major development of infrastructure needed for transport purposes.

....

....

....

....

....

....

....

LANGUAGE TIP

Start your final paragraph with a phrase that prepares the reader for your conclusions because they are often the most interesting part. Use *In conclusion, ... To conclude, ... Ultimately, ... Given these advantages and disadvantages, it can be concluded that ....*

7   The development of **plastics** and synthetic fibres has provided many advantages in modern life. However, there are disadvantages to their use and disposal. Write a brief analysis of the issues involved in the continued development of polymers and plastics. Use the headings and concepts in the Language Focus box in Exercise 20.2 to help you structure your analysis and argument.

Introduction

....

....

....

....

....

....

Advantages – the usefulness of polymers (one or two main examples)

....

....

....

....

....

....

Disadvantages of the use of polymers (e.g. waste disposal, plastic in the oceans)

....

....

....

....

....

Conclusion

....

....

....

....

....

Chapter 21

Experimental design and separation techniques

IN THIS CHAPTER YOU WILL:

Science skills:

- understand how various separation techniques are used

- understand and describe the steps involved in paper chromatography, and design an experiment using the technique.

English skills:

- form the nouns that can be derived from verbs describing various processes in chemistry

- practise the use of prepositions in relative clauses.

Exercise 21.1 Practical separation methods

IN THIS EXERCISE YOU WILL:

Science skills:

- look at some of the practical separation methods used in chemistry.

English skills:

- practise and apply some key terms related to separation techniques.

KEY WORD

residue: the solid left behind in the filter paper after filtration has taken place

1   a   Complete the table with the missing words. The first row has been done for you.

Verb	-ing form	Noun – name of process	Noun – product of process
to condense	condensing	condensation	the condensate
to separate	....	....	
to distil	....	....	....
to filter	....	filtration	the filtrate
to precipitate	....	....	the precipitate
....	neutralising	....	
to calculate	....	....	
....	....	titration	the titre
to oxidise	....	oxidation	
to reduce	....	....	
....	purifying	....	

LANGUAGE TIP

Remember that most English verbs have only four or five forms: infinitive (*react*), present form with 's' (*it reacts*), past simple form (*reacted/gave*), past participle (*reacted/ given*), and -*ing* form (*reacting*).

b   The method of filtration is illustrated in Figure 21.1.

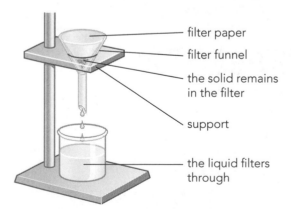

- filter paper
- filter funnel
- the solid remains in the filter
- support
- the liquid filters through

Figure 21.1: The method of filtration.

Complete the following passage describing a precipitation reaction, followed by a filtration, using the correct form(s) of the verb given at the start of each paragraph.

Verb: precipitate

Carbon dioxide was bubbled through limewater solution. A .... reaction occurred, in which calcium carbonate was formed.

This .... was a white solid, which made the limewater appear 'milky'.

Verb: filter

The white solid was separated from the liquid by ....

The mixture was .... by pouring it into a filter funnel containing a filter paper. The solid **residue** remained in the filter paper. The liquid .... passed through the filter paper and was collected in a flask.

LANGUAGE FOCUS

Remember when to use the -*ing* form of a verb.

1   As a noun, so:

   •   When you want to use a verb as the subject of a sentence:

       Filtering a solution removes unwanted sediment.

       Separating a pure substance from contaminants is important.

   •   After a preposition:

       He's very interested in learning more about chemistry.

       Scientists are looking into mining the ocean floor for important metals.

   •   After some verbs, e.g. *avoid, begin, start, stop, try*:

       We tried calculating the rate of reaction.

       We stopped recording data for the experiment when the reaction ended.

2   As a shorter version of something longer, so:

   •   After *when*, to mean 'when you are / it is / they are', etc.:

       When calculating the average titration value, remember not to count the first rough value.

   •   After a noun or *something, everything, anything*, etc., to mean 'who is/ are' or 'which is/are':

       Scientists studying battery technology want to find ones that recharge quickly.

       The space-probe currently travelling to Mars will chemically analyse rock samples.

c   Complete the paragraph using the *-ing* form of the verbs in the box. There is one word you do not need.

to distil   to estimate   to filter   to precipitate   to purify

to separate   to titrate

There are several different methods used for .... and .... substances in chemistry. Purifying water for domestic use involves some of these processes. .... small particles from river water can be achieved using sand beds. Other impurities can be removed by .... them by the addition of precipitators that make them insoluble. The acidity of a water supply can be tested by .... the water with a standard alkali solution. In some countries clean water must be prepared .... seawater.

Exercise 21.2 Separating seawater by distillation

IN THIS EXERCISE YOU WILL:

Science skills:

• discuss the nature of the process of simple distillation.

English skills:

• use prepositions with relative causes to give precise scientific information.

KEY WORD

distillation: the process of boiling a liquid and then condensing the vapour produced back into a liquid; used to purify liquids and to separate liquids from solutions

Water is a good solvent. The oceans cover a large part of the surface of our planet, and they contain dissolved salts. The water in our bodies also contains many dissolved chemicals (solutes). These help our bodies to work properly.

2   Figure 21.2 illustrates the simple **distillation** of seawater. This process is used to purify water.

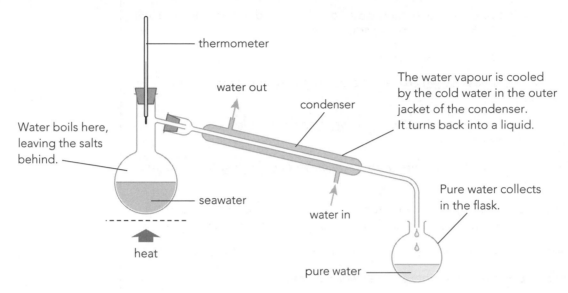

Figure 21.2: The simple distillation of seawater.

Use information from the diagram to write a short paragraph describing how the process works. Start with what happens in the distillation flask, then in the condenser, and finally in the collecting flask. Include the following words in your paragraph:

boiling point   cold water   condenses   distillate

flask   flows   higher   lower   outer jacket

....

....

....

....

....

....

....

....

....

....

LANGUAGE FOCUS

When you define or describe in chemistry, you often need to use phrases such as: *at which, by which, in which, to whom, with whom*:

The temperature <u>at which</u> water boils is 100 °C.

Filtration is the process <u>by which</u> we separate insoluble substances from a suspension.

Paula Hammond has created polymers <u>in which</u> the molecules reorganise themselves.

Rosalind Franklin was the scientist <u>with whom</u> Raymond Gosling took the first image of DNA.

This is because, although you can put a preposition at the end of a sentence in conversation, it is not considered formal enough for scientific writing:

The melting point is the temperature that something melts <u>at</u>. = conversation

The melting point is the temperature <u>at which</u> something melts. = scientific writing

Replace *that* with *which* (or *whom*, for people) and move the preposition in front of it.

---

3 **a**   Complete the following sentences by circling the correct prepositions.

  i   Simple distillation is a method **by / at / to** which a liquid solvent can be separated from dissolved solutes with much higher boiling points.

  ii   Fractional distillation is the industrial process **to / in / at** which the different fractions are separated according to their different boiling points.

  iii   John Dalton is the person **by / at / to** whom the first modern ideas of atomic theory are credited.

  iv   A filter funnel is the apparatus **to / in / at** which the folded filter paper is placed for filtration.

  v   The freezing point of a substance is the temperature **to / in / at** which a liquid solidifies.

  vi   Rutherford was the Nobel prize-winning scientist **at / by / with** whom Geiger and Marsden worked on the structure of the atom.

  b   Complete these sentences using *which* or *whom* and a suitable ending to the sentence.

  i   Carl Bosch is the person with .... Fritz Haber ....

  ....

  ii   A volumetric pipette is the apparatus with ....

  ....

iii   In an acid–alkali titration the end point is the point at ....

....

iv   Group VII of the Periodic Table is the group in ....

....

v   The boiling point of a liquid is the temperature at ....

....

vi   Barium nitrate solution is the reagent with ....

....

Exercise 21.3 Chromatography

IN THIS EXERCISE YOU WILL:

Science skills:

*   understand the basis and practice of paper chromatography, and design an experimental method using the technique.

English skills:

*   develop techniques for recording and note taking, and for writing methods.

4   The paper chromatogram in Figure 21.3 compares two coloured mixtures, X and Y.

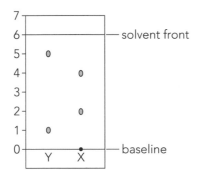

Figure 21.3: Chromatography of coloured mixtures X and Y.

a   State two factors which determine the distance a substance travels up the paper.

....

b Do mixtures X and Y have any components in common? Explain your answer.

....

....

5 Read the following sentences and circle the correct meaning (**A** or **B**).

a If the baseline is drawn in ink, your result may be spoilt by the ink dissolving in the solvent.

    A Use ink to draw the line.

    B Don't use ink to draw the line.

b The solvent rises up the paper taking the spots with it, so unless you stop the experiment before the solvent reaches the top, you may lose spots at the top edge of the paper.

    A Stop the experiment before the solvent reaches the top.

    B Don't stop the experiment until the solvent reaches the top.

c The spots separate as they move. However, if two substances in the sample have the same solubility they will move together and not separate.

    A You want the spots to separate, so use a solvent where solubilities are different.

    B You want the spots to separate, so use a solvent where solubilities are the same.

d The samples are spotted on the paper. However, unless the spots are very small, they will spread too much.

    A Make the spots very small.

    B Don't use very small spots.

e The substances present in the mixture move up the chromatography paper according to their solubility. However, if a substance is insoluble it will stay on the baseline.

    A Use a solvent in which all the sample is soluble.

    B Use a solvent in which not all the sample is soluble.

Now read the advice and warnings you have circled again. Which of your answers (**a–e**) give the correct advice?

....

> ### LANGUAGE TIP
>
> *Unless* often introduces a warning or advice. Its meaning is similar to 'If (you) don't…'.
>
> *If you <u>don't use</u> absorbent paper, chromatography won't work*
>
> = *<u>Unless</u> you <u>use</u> absorbent paper, chromatography won't work.*
>
> The meaning of both example sentences = 'Use absorbent paper.'

LANGUAGE FOCUS

When you work in a lab, read a scientific book, or listen to a science lesson or podcast, it is important to take notes quickly and efficiently. It is also important to keep all the key words and data, but there are other things you can eliminate, shorten or change to a symbol.

1   Eliminate: words like *is*, *are* and *the* can usually be eliminated from notes.

   The spots are initially dark blue. → *spots initially dark blue*

   The paper is held vertically. → *paper held vertically*

   Some people also use '–' for *is* or *are*:

   The spots are initially blue. → *spots – initially blue*

2   Shorten: words like *with*, *very* and *because* can be shortened; numbers become numerals:

   Hold the paper with care. → *Hold paper w care.*

   Three drops do not separate, because they are similar. → *3 drops don't separate bcz similar*

3   Use symbols: words like *or*, *more* and *for example* can be replaced by a symbol:

   bottom or top → *bottom / top*

   three or more → *3+*

   such as, *for instance*, *for example* → *e.g.*

6   Fadel took revision notes summarising paper chromatography, but water fell on his notes. What did his missing notes say? Use your knowledge and information from the Coursebook to help you complete his notes.

Paper chromatography:

1   originally developed as method fr separating soluble pigments (coloured substances e.g. dyes & inks) using filter paper

2   separating 2 or + dissolved solids in solution possible

3   substances separate according to solubility in solvent

4   1 drop concentrated solution – usually placed on pencil line (the baseline/origin) near bottom edge of strip of chromatography paper: pencil used to draw the line – doesn't dissolve & interfere w the separation

5   paper then dipped in solvent

6   ....

7   ....

....

8   ....

....

9   ....

....

10 ....

....

7   Saffron is a yellow food colouring that comes from crocus flowers; it tastes good, but is expensive. Harjit finds cheap, very brightly coloured saffron at a market. Harjit thinks it may contain a harmful additive. He has some real saffron at home, which is much paler in colour.

Design an experimental method to compare the two samples of saffron to see if an artificial colour has been added to the cheap saffron. Use the knowledge you have gained from your practical work and the examples of experimental planning from previous chapters throughout this book to help you write the method.

....

....

....

....

....

....

....

....

....

....

....

> Chapter 22
Chemical analysis

IN THIS CHAPTER YOU WILL:

Science skills:

- see how analytical tests can help evaluate the chemical content of different types of chemical sample
- understand and describe the methodology of tests for a range of chemical ions and compounds.

English skills:

- familiarise yourself with words for sequencing test instructions and procedures
- discover and practise how test results can be presented and discussed.

Exercise 22.1 Analysing mineral water

IN THIS EXERCISE YOU WILL:

Science skills:

- investigate how analytical tests can be used to determine the quality of mineral water.

English skills:

- learn how command words *evaluate*, *compare* and *explain* help you write about chemical tests.

1   Figure 22.1 shows the label on a bottle of Harcourt Mineral Water.

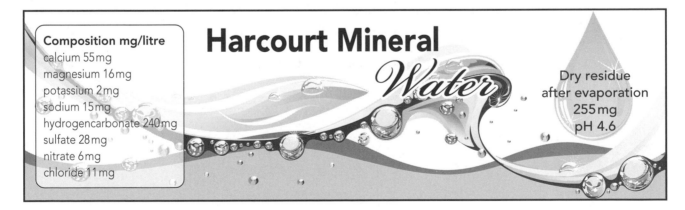

Composition mg/litre
calcium 55 mg
magnesium 16 mg
potassium 2 mg
sodium 15 mg
hydrogencarbonate 240 mg
sulfate 28 mg
nitrate 6 mg
chloride 11 mg

Harcourt Mineral Water

Dry residue after evaporation 255 mg
pH 4.6

Figure 22.1: The ionic contents of a mineral water.

LANGUAGE FOCUS

You have seen in earlier chapters that it is important to understand command words, in order to understand what you have to do for a specific question or task. Understanding command words such as *evaluate*, *compare* and *explain* will also help you decide what language (words, phrases, structures) you should use.

Evaluate: to judge or calculate the quality, importance, amount or value of something. You can use words such as *whereas*, *although* and *rather than*, as well as superlatives (*the lowest*, *the greatest*, *the best*, etc.), to consider the advantages and disadvantages.

Compare: to identify/comment on similarities and/or differences between two or more things. Phrase such as *not as many as*, *as much as* and *less… than*, and comparative adjectives are useful.

Explain: to say why/how things happen (see Chapter 2). Words such as *first*, *then*, *next*, *because of* and *due to* help here.

a i Compare two methods you could use to confirm that the pH of the water was 4.6.

....

....

....

ii Explain how you would confirm the presence of sodium ions in the mineral water.

....

....

....

....

iii Evaluate the two general methods available to test for the presence of metal ions in solution.

....

....

....

....

....

....

....

iv Explain how you could carefully confirm the amount of dry residue given at the end of the label.

....

....

....

....

....

....

....

Exercise 22.2 Flame tests for metals

IN THIS EXERCISE YOU WILL:

Science skills:

- describe how to perform a flame test to identify the presence of positive metal ions.

English skills:

- use sequencers when describing the steps in an experiment.

LANGUAGE FOCUS

When you describe an experiment or give instructions, it helps understanding if you use words to show the sequence. These useful words (sequencers) include *first (of all)*, *next*, *then*, *after that* and *finally*:

First, set the level of acid solution in the burette to zero before the titration.

Use *next*, *then* or *after that* to introduce the steps in your experiment or instructions. In this context they all mean the same thing.

Then open the tap and carefully add the acid to the alkali in the flask.

Next, open the tap and carefully add the acid to the alkali in the flask.

Use *finally* to introduce the last step in your experiment or instructions.

Finally, stop adding acid immediately after the indicator changes colour.

2   a   The four pictures **A–D** in Figure 22.2 show the steps involved in carrying out a flame test, but they are not given in the correct order.

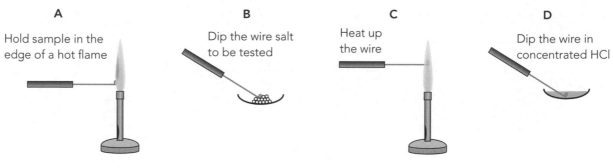

Figure 22.2: Method for the flame test.

Reorder the steps by writing the correct letter **A**, **B**, **C** or **D** in each box.

1 ☐   2 ☐   3 ☐   4 ☐

b   Write the complete instructions for carrying out the flame test on a salt sample. Use Figure 22.2 and the words in the Language Focus box to help you.

First of all, ...

....

....

....

....

....

....

Exercise 22.3 Reactivity of the halogens

IN THIS EXERCISE YOU WILL:

Science skills:

• investigate tests for halogens based on their reactivity.

English skills:

• develop your skills writing conclusions for experiments.

3 The halogens chlorine, bromine and iodine differ in their ability to displace another halogen from a solution of its salt. The following notes on an experiment were taken by a student. They include observations from the tests carried out. The halogens were provided as solutions in water, and the test was to add the halogen to the salt solution (see Figure 22.3). The solutions provided were potassium chloride, potassium bromide and potassium iodide.

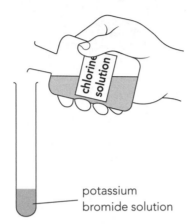

potassium
bromide solution

Figure 22.3: Testing the reactivity of the halogens.

Results – notes:

- **KCl** solution with bromine or iodine solutions – no change to colourless solution

- **KBr** solution with iodine solution – no change to colourless solution – no colour in hexane layer at end; KBr solution with chlorine solution – solution colourless to brown

- **KI** solution with chlorine or bromine water – solution colourless to brown in both cases

a Read the student's notes carefully, then draw a table of the results of the experiment. Think what you will need to include.

    i How many columns would your table need? ....

    ii How many rows would your table need? ....

    iii What will you write at the top of each column?

    ....

    iv What will you write at the left-hand end of each row?

    ....

    v What information will you write in each cell in the table?

    ....

> **LANGUAGE TIP**
>
> The individual boxes in tables are called *cells*. The vertical lines of cells are called *columns*. The horizontal lines of cells are called *rows*.

vi   If there is no change, what will you write in the corresponding cell?

....

Now draw your table in the space provided and enter the observations from the notes.

b   Use the results to complete the boxes in the diagram, placing the halogens tested in order of increasing reactivity.

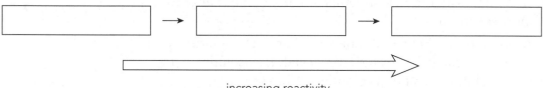

increasing reactivity

c   i   Reorder the sentences to form the concluding paragraphs of two different discussions. Each conclusion consists of three sentences. Use your knowledge of chemistry and the information in the Language Focus box in Exercise 20.3 to help.

   A   However, the use of an ion exchanger in the water system of a building can remove this problem.

   B   Consequently, the best approach to reduce these problems is to ban the use of single-use plastic packaging entirely.

   C   Therefore, in order to protect buildings and homes from the possibility of burst water pipes and flooding, such exchangers should be installed automatically in hard-water areas.

   D   To conclude, the use of polymers in packaging has brought great advantages.

   E   In conclusion, the presence of calcium salts in the water supply of hard-water areas eventually gives rise to the blockage of hot-water pipes with limescale.

F However, the fact that so much packaging, particularly single-use plastic, is non-biodegradable means that it poses an immense environmental problem.

Concluding paragraph 1: sentences ..../.............../...............

Concluding paragraph 2: sentences ..../.............../...............

ii Now write your own conclusion, comparing the trend in reactivity of the elements in Group VII with the metals of Group I (see Chapter 13; Exercise 13.3).

....

....

....

....

....

....

....

....

....

....

Exercise 22.4 Analysis of an alloy

IN THIS EXERCISE YOU WILL:

Science skills:

- investigate tests for anions and cations.

English skills:

- develop the ability to write a sequence of experimental instructions.

KEY WORD

cation: a positive ion which would be attracted to the cathode in electrolysis

4 Magnalium is an alloy of aluminium (95%) and magnesium (5%). The composition of magnalium can be tested analytically. Figure 22.5 shows the reactions carried out on a sample in the laboratory to confirm its composition.

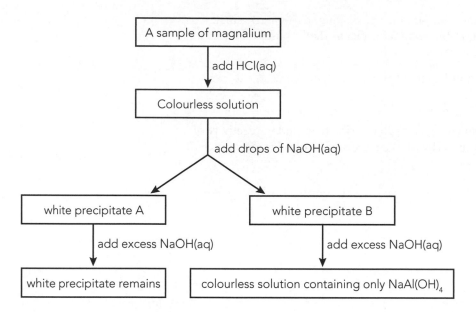

Figure 22.4: Analytical test on magnalium.

a   Write instructions for carrying out an analytical test on magnalium. Use the flowchart in Figure 22.4 to help you.

Step 1: First of all, ...

....

....

....

....

....

....

....

....

....

....

....

....

b State the formulae of the two **cations** present in the colourless solution at the start of the test.

....

....

....

....

....

....

....

....

....

c Identify the two white precipitates formed in the tests.

precipitate **A**: ....

 precipitate **B**: ....

d The following paragraph describes the tests for halide ions.

> The test for halide ions (chloride (Cl^-), bromide (Br^-) and iodide (I^-)) is the formation of a precipitate when a solution of acidified silver nitrate is added. The test produces different colours of precipitate: a chloride forms a white precipitate, a bromide forms a cream precipitate, and an iodide forms a yellow precipitate.

Explain how you would test for the halide ions present in the colourless solution from dissolving magnalium in acid. Use the information above to help you. You should also include the result of the test and the identity of the anions (negative ions) present.

....

....

....

....

....

....

....

> Glossary

Command Words

Below are the Cambridge International definitions for command words which may be used in exams. The information in this section is taken from the Cambridge IGCSE™ Chemistry syllabus (0620/0971) for examination from 2023. You should always refer to the appropriate syllabus document for the year of your examination to confirm the details and for more information. The syllabus document is available on the Cambridge International website www.cambridgeinternational.org.

analyse: examine in detail to show meaning, identify elements and the relationship between them

calculate: work out from given facts, figures or information

compare: identify/comment on similarities and/or differences

consider: review and respond to given information

contrast: identify/comment on differences

deduce: conclude from available information

define: give precise meaning

demonstrate: show how or give an example

describe: state the points of a topic / give characteristics and main features

determine: establish an answer using the information available

discuss: write about issue(s) or topic(s) in depth in a structured way

evaluate: judge or calculate the quality, importance, amount, or value of something

examine: investigate closely, in detail

explain: set out purposes or reasons / make the relationships between things evident / provide why and/or how and support with relevant evidence

give: produce an answer from a given source or recall/memory

identify: name/select/recognise

justify: support a case with evidence/argument

predict: suggest what may happen based on available information

show (that): provide structured evidence that leads to a given result

sketch: make a simple freehand drawing showing the key features, taking care over proportions

state: express in clear terms

suggest: apply knowledge and understanding to situations where there are a range of valid responses in order to make proposals / put forward considerations

Key Words

acid: a substance that dissolves in water, producing $H^+(aq)$ ions – a solution of an acid turns litmus red and has a pH below 7
Acids act as proton donors

acid–base titration: a method of quantitative chemical analysis where an acid is added slowly to a base until it has been neutralised

activation energy (E_a): the minimum energy required to start a chemical reaction – for a reaction to take place the colliding particles must possess at least this amount of energy

addition reaction: a reaction in which a simple molecule adds across the carbon–carbon double bond of an alkene

alcohols: a series of organic compounds containing the functional group –OH and with the general formula $C_nH_{2n+1}OH$

alkali metals: elements in Group I of the Periodic Table; they are the most reactive group of metals

alkalis: soluble bases that produce OH^- (aq) ions in water – a solution of an alkali turns litmus blue and has a pH above 7

alkanes: a series of hydrocarbons with the general formula C_nH_{2n+2}; they are saturated compounds as they have only single bonds between carbon atoms in their structure

alkenes: a series of hydrocarbons with the general formula C_nH_{2n}; they are unsaturated molecules as they have a C=C double bond somewhere in the chain.

alloys: mixtures of elements (usually metals) designed to have properties useful for a particular purpose, e.g. solder (an alloy of tin and lead) has a low melting point

anode: the electrode in any type of cell at which oxidation (the loss of electrons) takes place – in electrolysis it is the positive electrode

atmosphere: the layer of air and water vapour surrounding the Earth

base: a substance that neutralises an acid, producing a salt and water as the only products; bases act as proton acceptors

bauxite: the major ore of aluminium; a form of aluminium oxide, Al_2O_3

blast furnace: a furnace for extracting metals (particularly iron) by reduction with carbon that uses hot air blasted in at the base of the furnace to raise the temperature

boiling: the process of change from liquid to gas at the boiling point of the substance; a condition under which gas bubbles are able to form within a liquid – gas molecules escape from the body of a liquid, not just from its surface

bond energy: the energy required to break a particular type of covalent bond

carboxylic acids: a homologous series of organic compounds containing the functional group –COOH (–CO_2H), with the general formula $C_nH_{2n+1}COOH$

catalyst: a substance that increases the rate of a chemical reaction but itself remains unchanged at the end of the reaction

cathode: the electrode in any type of cell at which reduction (the gain of electrons) takes place; in electrolysis it is the negative electrode

cation: a positive ion which would be attracted to the cathode in electrolysis

ceramic: material such as pottery from inorganic chemicals by high-temperature processing

chemical reaction (change): a change in which a new substance is formed

clean dry air: containing no water vapour and only the gases which are always present in the air

closed system: a system where none of the reactants or products can escape the reaction mixture or the container where the reaction is taking place

collision theory: a theory which states that a chemical reaction takes place when particles of the reactants collide with sufficient energy to initiate the reaction

combustion: a chemical reaction in which a substance reacts with oxygen – the reaction is exothermic

compound ion: an ion made up of several different atoms covalently bonded together and with an overall charge

compound: a substance formed by the chemical combination of two or more elements in fixed proportions

condensation reaction: a reaction where two or more substances combine together to make a larger compound, and a small molecule is eliminated (given off)

corrosion: the process that takes place when metals and alloys are chemically attacked by oxygen, water or any other substances found in their immediate environment

covalent bonding: chemical bonding formed by the sharing of one or more pairs of electrons between two atoms

cryolite: sodium aluminium fluoride (Na_3AlF_6), an ore of aluminium used in the extraction of aluminium to lower the operating temperature of the electrolytic cell. Now replaced by synthetic sodium aluminium fluoride produced from the common mineral fluorite

crystallisation: the process of forming crystals from a saturated solution

dehydration: a chemical reaction in which water is removed from a compound

dependent variable: the variable which is measured during a scientific investigation

diffusion: the process by which different fluids mix as a result of the random motions of their particles

displacement reaction: a reaction in which a more reactive element displaces a less reactive element from a solution of its salt

displayed formula: a representation of the structure of a compound which shows all the atoms and bonds in the molecule

dissolving: a process that produces a solution of a solid or gas in a liquid, e.g. when sugar dissolves in water

distillate: the liquid collected in the receiving flask during distillation

distillation: the process of boiling a liquid and then condensing the vapour produced back into a liquid; used to purify liquids and to separate liquids from solutions

electrical conductivity: the ability to conduct electricity

electrical conductor: a substance that conducts electricity but is not chemically changed in the process

electrolysis: the breakdown of an ionic compound, molten or in aqueous solution, by the use of electricity

electrolyte: an ionic compound that will conduct electricity when it is molten or dissolved in water; electrolytes will not conduct electricity when solid

electronic configuration: a shorthand method of describing the arrangement of electrons within the electron shells (or energy levels) of an atom; also referred to as electronic structure

element: a substance which cannot be further divided into simpler substances by chemical methods; all the atoms of an element contain the same number of protons

end point: the point in a titration when the indicator just changes colour showing that the reaction is complete

endothermic change: a process or chemical reaction which takes in heat from the surroundings. ΔH for an endothermic change has a positive value.

enthalpy (H): the thermal (heat) content of a system

enthalpy change (ΔH): the heat change during the course of a reaction (also known as heat of reaction); can be either exothermic (a negative value) or endothermic (a positive value)

enzymes: protein molecules that act as biological catalysts

evaporation: a process occurring at the surface of a liquid, involving the change of state from a liquid into a vapour at a temperature below the boiling point

exothermic changes: a process or chemical reaction in which heat energy is produced and released to the surroundings. ΔH for an exothermic change has a negative value

fermentation: a reaction carried out using a living organism, usually a yeast or bacteria, to produce a useful chemical compound; most usually refers to the production of ethanol

fertiliser: a substance added to the soil to replace essential elements lost when crops are harvested, which enables crops to grow faster and increases the yield

filtrate: the liquid that passes through the filter paper during filtration

filtration: the separation of a solid from a liquid, using a fine filter paper which does not allow the solid to pass through

fluid: a gas or a liquid; they are able to flow

fractional distillation: a method of distillation using a fractionating column, used to separate liquids with different boiling points

fractions (from distillation): the different mixtures that distil over at different temperatures during fractional distillation

functional group: the atom or group of atoms responsible for the characteristic reactions of a compound

galvanising: the protection of iron and steel objects by coating with a layer of zinc

giant covalent structures: a substance where large numbers of atoms are held together by covalent bonds forming a strong lattice structure

greenhouse gas: a gas that absorbs thermal energy reflected from the surface of the Earth, stopping it escaping the atmosphere

groups: vertical columns of the Periodic Table containing elements with similar chemical properties; atoms of elements in the same group have the same number of electrons in their outer energy levels

Haber process: the industrial manufacture of ammonia by the reaction of nitrogen with hydrogen in the presence of an iron catalyst

halogens: elements in Group VII of the Periodic Table – generally the most reactive group of non-metals

hematite: the major ore of iron, iron(III) oxide

homologous series: a family of similar compounds with similar chemical properties due to the presence of the same functional group

hydrated salts: salts whose crystals contain combined water (*water of crystallisation*) as part of the structure

hydration: the addition of the elements of water across a carbon–carbon double bond: H– adds to one carbon, and –OH to the other

hydrocarbons: organic compounds which contain carbon and hydrogen only; the alkanes and alkenes are two series of hydrocarbons

independent variable: the variable that is altered during a scientific investigation

indicator: a substance which changes colour when added to acidic or alkaline solutions, e.g. litmus or thymolphthalein

insulator: a substance that does not conduct electricity

intermolecular forces: the weak attractive forces which act between molecules

ionic bonding: a strong electrostatic force of attraction between oppositely charged ions

ions: charged particles made from an atom, or group of atoms (compound ions), by the loss or gain of electrons

isomerism: the property shown by molecules which have the same molecular formula but different structures

isomers: compounds which have the same molecular formula but different structural arrangements of the atoms – they have different structural formulae

isotopes: atoms of the same element which have the same proton number but a different nucleon number; they have different numbers of neutrons in their nuclei; some isotopes are radioactive because their nuclei are unstable (radioisotopes)

kinetic particle theory: a theory which accounts for the bulk properties of the different states of matter in terms of the movement of particles (atoms or molecules) – the theory explains what happens during changes in physical state

limestone: a form of calcium carbonate ($CaCO_3$)

matter: anything that occupies space and has mass

metallic bonding: an electrostatic force of attraction between the mobile 'sea' of electrons and the regular array of positive metal ions within a solid metal

mixture: two or more substances mixed together but not chemically combined – the substances can be separated by physical means

molecule: a group of atoms held together by covalent bonds

monomer: a small molecule, such as ethene, which can be polymerised to make a polymer

neutralisation: a chemical reaction between an acid and a base to produce a salt and water only; summarised by the ionic equation $H^+(aq) + OH^-(aq) \rightarrow H_2O(l)$

noble gases: elements in Group VIII – a group of stable, very unreactive gases

nucleus: (of an atom) the central region of an atom that is made up of the protons and neutrons of the atom; the electrons orbit around the nucleus in different 'shells' or 'energy levels'

ore: a naturally occurring mineral from which a metal can be extracted

oxidation number: a number given to show whether an element has been oxidised or reduced; the oxidation number of a simple ion is simply the charge on the ion

oxidation: there are three definitions of oxidation:
i a reaction in which oxygen is added to an element or compound;
ii a reaction involving the loss of electrons from an atom, molecule or ion;
iii a reaction in which the oxidation state of an element is increased

oxidising agent: a substance which oxidises another substance during a redox reaction

period: a horizontal row of the Periodic Table

periodic change: pattern in which certain physical and chemical properties repeat themselves regularly as we follow a sequence of elements with increasing atomic number

Periodic Table: a table of elements arranged in order of increasing proton number (atomic number) to show the similarities of the chemical elements with related electron configurations

petroleum (or crude oil): a fossil fuel formed underground over many millions of years by conditions of high pressure and temperature acting on the remains of dead sea creatures

pH scale: a scale running from below 0 to 14, used for expressing the acidity or alkalinity of a solution; a neutral solution has a pH of 7

photosynthesis: the chemical process by which plants synthesise glucose from atmospheric carbon dioxide and water giving off oxygen as a by-product: the energy required for the process is captured from sunlight by chlorophyll molecules in the green leaves of the plants

physical change: a change in the physical state of a substance or the physical nature of a situation that does not involve a change in the chemical substance(s) present

plastics: polymers that can be moulded or shaped by the action of heat and pressure

pollutants: substances, often harmful, which are added to another substance

polymer: a substance consisting of very large molecules made by polymerising a large number of repeating units or monomers

polymerisation: the chemical reaction in which molecules (monomers) join together to form a long-chain polymer

precipitation: the sudden formation of a solid when either two solutions are mixed or a gas is bubbled into a solution

reaction pathway diagram (energy level diagram): a diagram that shows the energy levels of the reactants and products in a chemical reaction and shows whether the reaction is exothermic or endothermic

reaction rate: a measure of how fast a reaction takes place

reactivity: the ease with which a chemical substance takes part in a chemical reaction

redox reaction: a reaction involving both reduction and oxidation

reducing agent: a substance which reduces another substance during a redox reaction

reduction: there are three definitions of reduction:
i a reaction in which oxygen is removed from a compound;
ii a reaction involving the gain of electrons by an atom, molecule or ion;
iii a reaction in which the oxidation state of an element is decreased

relative atomic mass (A_r): the average mass of naturally occurring atoms of an element on a scale where the carbon-12 atom has a mass of exactly 12 units

relative formula mass (M_r): the sum of all the relative atomic masses of all the atoms present in a 'formula unit' of a substance

relative molecular mass (M_r): the sum of all the relative atomic masses of the atoms present in a molecule

residue: the solid left behind in the filter paper after filtration has taken place

reversible reaction: a chemical reaction that can go either forwards or backwards, depending on the conditions

rust: a loose, orange–brown, flaky layer of hydrated iron(III) oxide, $Fe_2O_3 \cdot xH_2O$, found on the surface of iron or steel

rusting: the corrosion of iron and steel to form rust (hydrated iron(III) oxide)

sacrificial protection: a method of rust protection involving the attachment of blocks of a metal more reactive than iron to a structure; this metal is corroded rather than the iron or steel structure

salts: ionic compounds made by the neutralisation of an acid with a base (or alkali), e.g. copper(II) sulfate and potassium nitrate

saturated hydrocarbons: hydrocarbon molecules in which all the carbon–carbon bonds are single covalent bonds

slag: a molten mixture of impurities, mainly calcium silicate, formed in the blast furnace

solubility: a measure of how much of a solute dissolves in a solvent at a particular temperature

solvent front: the moving boundary of the liquid solvent that moves up the paper during chromatography

strong acid: an acid that is completely ionised when dissolved in water – this produces the highest possible concentration of $H^+(aq)$ ions in solution, e.g. hydrochloric acid

transition metals (transmission elements): elements from the central region of the Periodic Table – they are hard, strong, dense metals that form compounds that are often coloured

universal indicator: a mixture of indicators that has different colours in solutions of different pH

unsaturated hydrocarbons: hydrocarbons whose molecules contain at least one carbon–carbon double or triple bond

water of crystallisation: water included in the structure of certain salts as they crystallise, e.g. copper(II) sulfate pentahydrate ($CuSO_4 \cdot 5H_2O$) contains five molecules of water of crystallisation per molecule of copper(II) sulfate

weak acid: an acid that is only partially dissociated into ions in water – usually this produces a low concentration of $H^+(aq)$ in the solution, e.g. ethanoic acid

word equation: a summary of a chemical reaction using the chemical names of the reactants and products

The Periodic Table of Elements

Key

atomic number
atomic symbol
name
relative atomic mass

Group

I	II	III	IV	V	VI	VII	VIII
							2 **He** helium 4

I	II												III	IV	V	VI	VII	VIII
1 **H** hydrogen 1																		
3 **Li** lithium 7	4 **Be** beryllium 9												5 **B** boron 11	6 **C** carbon 12	7 **N** nitrogen 14	8 **O** oxygen 16	9 **F** fluorine 19	10 **Ne** neon 20
11 **Na** sodium 23	12 **Mg** magnesium 24												13 **Al** aluminium 27	14 **Si** silicon 28	15 **P** phosphorus 31	16 **S** sulfur 32	17 **Cl** chlorine 35.5	18 **Ar** argon 40
19 **K** potassium 39	20 **Ca** calcium 40	21 **Sc** scandium 45	22 **Ti** titanium 48	23 **V** vanadium 51	24 **Cr** chromium 52	25 **Mn** manganese 55	26 **Fe** iron 56	27 **Co** cobalt 59	28 **Ni** nickel 59	29 **Cu** copper 64	30 **Zn** zinc 65		31 **Ga** gallium 70	32 **Ge** germanium 73	33 **As** arsenic 75	34 **Se** selenium 79	35 **Br** bromine 80	36 **Kr** krypton 84
37 **Rb** rubidium 85	38 **Sr** strontium 88	39 **Y** yttrium 89	40 **Zr** zirconium 91	41 **Nb** niobium 93	42 **Mo** molybdenum 96	43 **Tc** technetium –	44 **Ru** ruthenium 101	45 **Rh** rhodium 103	46 **Pd** palladium 106	47 **Ag** silver 108	48 **Cd** cadmium 112		49 **In** indium 115	50 **Sn** tin 119	51 **Sb** antimony 122	52 **Te** tellurium 128	53 **I** iodine 127	54 **Xe** xenon 131
55 **Cs** caesium 133	56 **Ba** barium 137	57–71 lanthanoids	72 **Hf** hafnium 178	73 **Ta** tantalum 181	74 **W** tungsten 184	75 **Re** rhenium 186	76 **Os** osmium 190	77 **Ir** iridium 192	78 **Pt** platinum 195	79 **Au** gold 197	80 **Hg** mercury 201		81 **Tl** thallium 204	82 **Pb** lead 207	83 **Bi** bismuth 209	84 **Po** polonium –	85 **At** astatine –	86 **Rn** radon –
87 **Fr** francium –	88 **Ra** radium –	89–103 actinoids	104 **Rf** rutherfordium –	105 **Db** dubnium –	106 **Sg** seaborgium –	107 **Bh** bohrium –	108 **Hs** hassium –	109 **Mt** meitnerium –	110 **Ds** darmstadtium –	111 **Rg** roentgenium –	112 **Cn** copernicium –		113 **Nh** nihonium –	114 **Fl** flerovium –	115 **Mc** moscovium –	116 **Lv** livermorium –	117 **Ts** tennessine –	118 **Og** oganesson –

lanthanoids

57 **La** lanthanum 139	58 **Ce** cerium 140	59 **Pr** praseodymium 141	60 **Nd** neodymium 144	61 **Pm** promethium –	62 **Sm** samarium 150	63 **Eu** europium 152	64 **Gd** gadolinium 157	65 **Tb** terbium 159	66 **Dy** dysprosium 163	67 **Ho** holmium 165	68 **Er** erbium 167	69 **Tm** thulium 169	70 **Yb** ytterbium 173	71 **Lu** lutetium 175

actinoids

89 **Ac** actinium –	90 **Th** thorium 232	91 **Pa** protactinium 231	92 **U** uranium 238	93 **Np** neptunium –	94 **Pu** plutonium –	95 **Am** americium –	96 **Cm** curium –	97 **Bk** berkelium –	98 **Cf** californium –	99 **Es** einsteinium –	100 **Fm** fermium –	101 **Md** mendelevium –	102 **No** nobelium –	103 **Lr** lawrencium –

The volume of one mole of any gas is $24\,dm^3$ at room temperature and pressure (r.t.p.).

> Acknowledgements

The authors and publishers acknowledge the following sources of copyright material and are grateful for the permissions granted.

Thanks to the following for permission to reproduce images:

Cover scotspencer/Getty Images; Haidar Mohammed Ali/Getty Images; Richard Harwood; Education Images/Getty Images